Rave Reviews for
Dan's Signature Franchise Method

OWN SUCCESS

"Since I started my new business last year, I've been thrilled. It's hard work, but I'm having the time of my life, and I finally have control over my career."

— *David C., Austin, Tx.*

"I never, never would have imagined myself owning a franchise. Until I met Dan, I thought franchises were burgers and fries. Now I own my own IT Services franchise."

— *Tony B., Seattle, Wa.*

"Dan helped me find a franchise that fit my budget and was a match for what interested me. I've been steadily profitable and continue to grow two years after I started my business. I'm enjoying my work life more than I ever did before."

— *Rachel T., Marietta, Ga.*

"Thanks for the help finding a franchise, Dan. It's been a great, profitable second career. It has made a big difference for my family."

— *Brian R., St. Louis, Mo.*

OWN SUCCESS

*A Proven Method to
Succeed in Business with a Franchise*

DAN CITRENBAUM

Leaders Press

Copyright © 2023 **Dan Citrenbaum**
Published in the United States by Leaders Press.
www.leaderspress.com

All rights reserved. No part of this book may be reproduced or transmitted in any form or by any means, electronic or mechanical, including photocopying, recording, or by an information storage and retrieval system – except by a reviewer who may quote brief passages in a review to be printed in a magazine or newspaper – without permission in writing from the publisher.

ISBN **978-1-63735-253-3** (pbk)
ISBN **978-1-63735-177-2** (ebook)

Library of Congress Control Number: **2022912811**

*This book is dedicated to
all the people who researched a franchise,
looked at the information they found,
put aside their fears,
and started a great business.*

You are the ones who win the future you want.

AUTHOR'S NOTE

I wrote this book to provide a tool to help people build lucrative careers as owners of successful businesses.

My own entrepreneurship journey has rewarded me in many ways. Not only have I succeeded financially, but, more importantly, business ownership has provided me with great personal fulfillment.

My interest in business ownership has allowed me to help thousands of people start and grow their own companies.

The people I have worked with have gained more control over their careers, achieved flexibility, developed the opportunity to assist their own clients, and, of course, forged a path to earn a larger income than they ever had before.

You will likely question the process of selecting a franchise and its effectiveness. Everybody does.

You will also have questions about franchises, perhaps like these:
- Can a franchise really help me earn the income I need?
- Are franchises risky?
- How do I find the franchise that is right for me?

I encourage you to ask tough questions throughout your entire investigation.

This book is organized to help you find the answers to your questions. The process is simple, straightforward, and thorough.

As I emphasize throughout, if you follow the process we recommend, you will discover being in business for yourself is less risky than you imagine. In these pages, you will learn about our time-tested approach that costs nothing but a little bit of your time.

If, after you finish reading the book
you want to start the process,
you can find a recorded version of the seminar I present here:

https://attendee.gotowebinar.com/register/8896813084148257539

If you decide to start the coaching process,
the first step is to complete our Entrepreneur Assessment,
which you can find at:

http://tinyurl.com/teoassessment

Curious? Then read on and learn how you too can minimize risk and benefit from owning a successful business—one that offers you financial security, an independent lifestyle, and control over your future.

INTRODUCTION

Can You Become an Entrepreneur?
(It's not as big a leap as you think)

You might naturally assume that since I've started seven businesses in my career, I must be comfortable with risk. As we will emphasize throughout these pages, beware of incorrect assumptions! Our entire method is designed to minimize risk.

When I was younger, I might have accepted a risky proposition. Back then, I didn't know any better. Fortunately, I haven't been that foolish in a long time. These days, when I consider a business opportunity, I won't give it a second glance unless the risk seems very low. After all, I'm not some executive in corporate America. My very own money and my very own future are on the line. I simply will not start a business unless the odds are clearly in my favor.

I've learned that I don't have to take a lot of risk to become a successful entrepreneur. And neither do you.

What do we mean by the word entrepreneur? While I see a multitude of dictionary definitions, to me an entrepreneur is someone willing to take advantage of a business opportunity. Note the absence of the word risk or bet.

The effective entrepreneur knows that to consistently win in business you have to minimize risk. Notice the two sides to this coin:

> *"Successful entrepreneurs*
> *seize opportunities*
> *while minimizing risk."*

During a career in which I've helped thousands of people evaluate, start and grow businesses, I find most people want to avoid risk.

Of course! Who would want risk? When I help someone become a business owner—usually for their first time—a lot of our work together is discussing how to reduce the risk as low as possible. To me, this is the essence of a true entrepreneur: A desire for the upside that comes from business ownership, but not the downside from reckless risk.

My expertise derives not only from being a franchise coach who has worked with thousands of business professionals over the years, but as a franchisee myself. While I had not intended to buy a franchise, the more I learned about franchises, the more I realized I should look for one of my own.

As I started to look for a franchise that would suit my own areas of expertise, I had my first epiphany. I realized I could find out everything I needed to know about the franchise to help me ensure success before investing one dollar. I bought my first franchise, in senior care, in 2010, and my second in 2018.

We will spend a good portion of this book discussing this critical balancing act for the budding entrepreneur: How can one become a business owner without accepting risk? The answer involves doing a lot of research before you make your investment.

First let's consider the general qualities you need as an entrepreneur:

- The ability to accurately assess your strengths
- A willingness to trust facts and information, rather than making decisions based on emotional swings or incorrect assumptions
- The ability to adjust the plan when necessary, without panic or exhilaration
- A strong work ethic
- Determination to get through those times that test your fortitude. No business starts and grows without a few challenges
- The ability to take responsibility. When you're the boss, you have to be willing to accept the responsibility as well as the credit. The buck stops with you.

The payoffs you get from accepting responsibility are the satisfaction and the financial rewards that come from success. Most entrepreneurs take particular satisfaction from creating a business that works and prospers. That is a powerful attraction.

In today's world, with wages stagnant, being your own boss can pay in more ways than one. Not only are you in charge of your own destiny, but you can reap the rewards of your own ingenuity and labor, plus get better security and financial stability.

In 1996, Thomas Stanley and William Danko wrote a book that was revolutionary in presenting a new way to see career planning and wealth. In *The Millionaire Next Door*, of all the valuable pieces of information the authors offer, the one that most caught my attention was:

> *"70% of all millionaires earned their fortune by owning their own businesses."*

We tend to think of movie stars or professional athletes when we think of millionaires, or in today's dollars, multimillionaires. When we consider wealthy businesspeople, we usually visualize the highly paid CEOs of public companies, say a Jeff Bezos or Bill Gates—people who founded what became large public companies.

But, Stanley and Danko point out, most millionaires never have that sort of fame or glamour. Most millionaires earn their money by starting their own businesses. And they're not high-profile businesses like Apple or Microsoft. We're talking about the small, almost anonymous businesses that cater to the demands in our economy. You likely drive by these businesses every day and never think twice about them.

In this book, I will refer often to my own experiences. And I'll tell you about the experiences of people I have worked with or supported as a coach: people who have started businesses and succeeded, sometimes beyond their most optimistic expectations.

We all have different paths to follow. For example, when I started out in business, my first job after earning my MBA was with an equipment leasing company. After two years there and another year working for a bank in their leasing department, I thought to myself: I can do this on my own and keep all the profits for myself.

I started my first company with a partner. I was only 26 years old and, while I didn't know much about running my own business, I had very low expenses—these were the days before marriage and children—and I was hungry for success. I took advantage of my experience in the business—what I call a period of apprenticeship—and used the contacts I made and my knowledge of this industry to start my own operation. And it was a success.

While the stereotype of an entrepreneur is of a young whippersnapper, starting your own business at mid-career has distinct advantages. Not only do you know a whole lot more about business, but you've also gained far more knowledge about the world, which can help you make gains a lot faster.

In business, the bald truth is there's never a time when you can sit back on your heels counting your earnings. Being in business for yourself requires always keeping an eye out for new opportunity, which sometimes means reinventing yourself to respond to changing conditions. That's exactly what I had to do after the crash of 2008 and the devastating credit crunch that followed.

After more than two decades in the leasing business, where I had excelled, having started two successful businesses in that field, the industry evaporated overnight, and I had to find another option, a new business in which I could make a good living. I saw this as a great opportunity to change up my career. Given the changes in the leasing industry, I was more than ready for something else.

My first step was to start researching. I talked to lots of people to learn ways I could use my experience in a new kind of business. After learning everything I could, I started on a new path as a franchise coach and, before long, a franchisee.

Knowing what I know now, I can say categorically,

> *"I would never start another business*
> *that wasn't a franchise—*
> *because no other type of business allows you to*
> *so fully manage your risk."*

JOB RISK vs. BUSINESS OWNERSHIP RISK

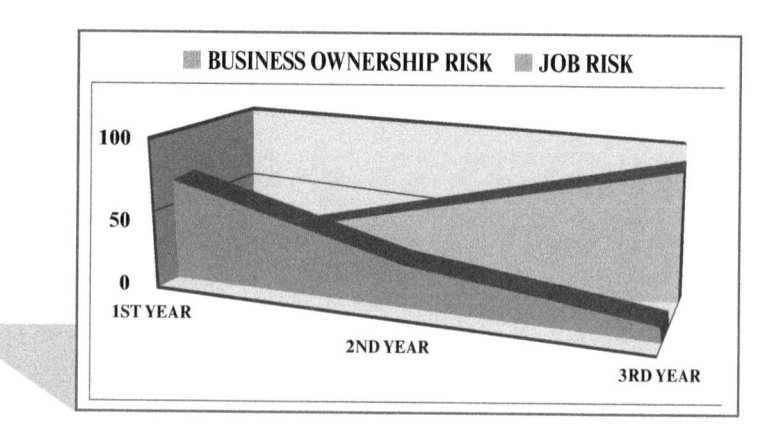

Are Wage Earners Ever Really Safe?

Most people think entrepreneurs are in a class of daredevils and what separates them from other people is they have spines of steel. They must be fearless, you would think, because they're willing to assume a great deal of risk. This assumption is the root of most people's reluctance to venture into business for themselves. But let's examine more closely the issue of risk.

You probably think starting a business entails taking far more risk than keeping your job. In one sense, a job is less risky. If you're hired on Monday, you probably won't be fired on Tuesday.

But if you look at the data, you will find the actual risk is not where you think it is. The real story may be counterintuitive, but it makes sense when you think about recent employment trends. We have greatly oversimplified the matter in the graph above, but the trend is clear and well supported by research.

The rising light gray bar shows that the longer you have a job, the higher the risk you face of losing it. And the dark gray bar shows that the longer you're in business for yourself, the lower the risk—i.e., the more likely you are to continue to survive and prosper. The fact is that the 21st century poses multiple risks for employees. Employees face a range of pitfalls, from wage stagnation to having your career redefined right out from under you. The writing has been on the wall for decades. Way back when I was in college, my faculty advisor spoke about future changes he expected to see in the workplace. I still remember his words:

*"Dan, your generation will need to
be prepared to reinvent themselves
every ten years, meaning, start over, learn new skills,
have new employers and new job titles, and
certainly, a new managerial track."*

This was quite a shift from the expectations of our parents, who often stayed with the same company for twenty years or more.

Looking at today's fast-paced, interconnected global economy, the idea of going ten years without change seems quaint. I recently heard a job-market expert say that mid-level and senior managers should prepare to reinvent and restart their careers every three years.

Clearly, there's no going back to the old days. If anything, the employment cycle is continuing to accelerate. Just look at how strongly corporate America has moved toward short-term independent contractors, a group with very little job security and no benefits.

How does this relate to risk and security? From the first day any one of us accepts a job, unless we are one of the very few, very fortunate ones, our days are numbered.

The Most Successful Employees Function Like Entrepreneurs

Think about that phrase for a moment. Every employee to some extent must exhibit the same imagination, work ethic, and hustle of an entrepreneur. To stay an employee, you actually have to become an entrepreneur, only you don't get to keep all the profit you produce. Your employer gets to determine your level of compensation, which is almost certainly less than the value you add to the bottom line.

For most companies, when you stay an employee, every month you work you are a month closer to the date you will be laid off or downsized or whatever euphemism they are using at the time. And that's what we mean when we say the longer you have a job, the higher your risk.

By contrast, someone who owns his or her own business can expect a lower risk over time. How can that be? Just compare a new business to the invention of a new machine, whose productivity improves as engineers work to perfect its functionality and efficiency. With a new business, the longer you operate, the more experienced your employees become and the better they can perform their jobs. You develop a loyal customer base, which is likely to continue to provide you a steady stream of business. Obviously, it's far less expensive to retain an existing customer than to find a new one.

While I would never claim the risk of business ownership ever goes down to zero, it certainly does decline over time.

So where is the risk? Everywhere! Risk exists in every possible career track, as an employee and as an owner. The mistake is in assuming it's always riskier to own your own business. I believe the key to success is to do your research before you start a business. That is the best way I know to truly reduce your risk.

PART ONE

as·sess
(verb)

To evaluate or estimate the nature, ability, or quality of.

synonyms:

evaluate
judge
gauge
rate
estimate
appraise
form an opinion of
check out
form an impression of
make up one's mind about
get the measure of
determine
weight up
analyze
informal size up

ONE

Is Starting Your Own Business Right for You?

If you've picked up this book, chances are you're thinking about changing careers. Maybe you don't like your job anymore, or you get the distinct impression that you're steps away from losing your position to downsizing, outsourcing or offshoring. As many of us will see for ourselves, mid- and senior-level corporate jobs are slowly being flushed down the drain of our fast-changing economy. Employees have little ability to change this trend.

Within these pages, we will show you ways to assess your present situation and become the force for change in your own career.

You may have already asked yourself the seminal question: Is this all there is? Maybe you've gone so far as to make lists of the types of jobs you dream of having, but how to get yourself from here to there feels out of your control. As a result, stuck in place, you're left with a range of concerns: Will my resumé stack up in today's job market? Will I trade one set of problems for another? Does my manager view me as obsolete?

Way back when you started your career, you had some vague idea where you wanted to end up. Now, after a few terrible bosses and some poor luck, you find yourself feeling stuck at a dead end. As a result, you're beginning to recognize the sad fact that your job has lost that spark, the one that used to make you excited to come to work every morning.

What a difference a decade or two can make in your mindset. But your job is not a life sentence. You're not stuck with an unsatisfying career until they pull the plug on you. To quote the character Howard Beale from the movie *Network* you can decide, "I'm not going to take this anymore!" Whether you're also "mad as hell" is another question entirely.

For our purposes, at this one moment in time, we encourage constructive—not destructive—thinking. There are steps you can take right now that can help you escape those frustrations, improve your working life and get the career you crave.

To underline the point a bit, take a short journey through the maze of pressures that have sucked the joy out of going to work.

The Job Pressures That Suck Out the Joy

In no particular order, they consist of:

Red Tape
Corporate America has its own brand of time-wasting, inflexible rules and regulations, including handbooks on what to wear and forms to fill out for myriad commonplace activities like vacations or expense accounts. It doesn't take much to transform these simple rules into ways corporations can control and harass you.

Office Politics
Who hasn't had a touchy boss or sketchy co-workers maneuver behind your back? You have no control over who you work with, whatsoever. Where do they find these jokers?!

Frustrations
It aggravates the best of us when HR departments don't return calls or when recruiters act as if they have never heard of you. You may be required to lead a project that you know is headed for disaster. And you can be sure your manager won't be the one taking the blame when the inevitable disappointment happens. You may not have control over who is on your team, but you will be responsible for a subordinate's poor performance.

Age Discrimination & Other Unfair Judgments
Many companies have an unwritten rule to lay off mid-career workers and unload those expensive salaries, regardless of how strong a contribution you still make. And you can see your time fast approaching.

Making More Money & Career Progress for Your Boss

Than for Yourself
Your boss takes credit for your accomplishments, and you can't seem to figure out how to get out from under his or her yoke.

Unreasonable Demands
Sure, bosses play favorites, but do you have to tolerate the boss's refusal to ever give an inch, often changing deadlines and reducing your resources while still expecting a perfect result?

Though the above list may sound like petty complaints, they can add up to a life of frustration and unhappiness.

The Connection Between Control & Happiness
As the quality of your career suffers, your life may feel increasingly out of your control. Numerous studies show the greater control you have over your day-to-day decision-making in your job, the happier you are, not only as a worker but in your life overall.

Research from such esteemed journals as the *Harvard Business Review* "clearly points to the power of choice and autonomy to drive not only employee happiness, but also motivation and performance."*

The choice-happiness quotient holds true for even seemingly small matters. The Gensler 2013 Workplace Study "found that knowledge workers whose companies allow them to decide when, where, and how they work were more likely to be satisfied with their jobs, performed better, and viewed their company as more innovative than competitors that didn't offer such choices."*

But you won't likely get that power to decide in corporate America.

You've probably read about the free-form offices in Silicon Valley, where employees get such perks as chef-made meals and great snacks, as well as fun-filled breaks of ping-pong or pool. This sounds fantastic, but they have the effect of encouraging workers to spend more time working, despite having no time for any personal life whatsoever.

As employees weigh the comparative importance of job satisfaction and income, experts have found more money alone does not necessarily improve job satisfaction. Beyond a certain level, more money doesn't really compensate for terrible conditions in the workplace. If you don't have any control at work, you're not likely to be happy, no matter how much money you make. This is why it can be worth your time to research alternatives to an unsatisfactory job.

The lesson:

*You're better off figuring out ways
to make a good living
while you maximize your ability to
gain greater control over your day-to-day life.
This is what will increase your happiness.*

While some companies get accolades for their great worker-friendly policies, we know full well that too many employers have abysmal records. Most notably, amid record corporate profits, wages have stagnated for decades, which has an impact on morale, as well as the pocketbook.

The reasons are legion for breaking your ties to corporate America and forging your career to match the vision you have for your life. After all, you only get one crack at it.

Find A Better Way

Read on to learn how to find another way, so you can gain:

- Increased income, more in line with the value you add
- Greater flexibility
- Better work-life balance
- Control over your career

- Independence

You're not likely to find the answers by merely switching jobs within the same company, or even moving across town to another company that turns out to have the same issues.

To get the change you crave, you have to sit in the driver's seat of your career. And the only way to see how far your skills can take you is to put them to work for yourself, rather than for some faceless corporation. There's no time like the present to strike out on your own with a business that belongs to you.

Get Started

Becoming the owner of your own business generally means following one of three paths:

1. Create your own independent concept, bringing your vision of a unique business to fruition.
2. Buy a business already active.
3. Buy a franchise and get a fully operational guidebook.

Maybe you've heard a bunch of stories about the high numbers of businesses that end up failing. We will discuss some of the truths and myths behind that sort of claim. If starting your own business looks like a hill that's too high to climb, connecting with a good franchise can be a great way to control your risk while getting all the benefits of entrepreneurship.

Of course, not all franchises are created equal. Like everything else in life, there are some winners and some real clunkers. Your own intelligence and ingenuity, as well as consulting with some smart, experienced experts, can help you find the right match for you. We'll get into the nuts and bolts about how to mine available resources in later pages.

Whether you choose to start your own business from scratch or buy a franchise, business ownership can put your career trajectory on an upward path once again.

Figure Out Your Priorities

Like beauty, the definition of success really is in the eye of the beholder.

The hardest part of all may be deciding what works for you. Too often promotions or a fattening paycheck don't alleviate that feeling of being stifled and unfulfilled. If that is the case, does the higher pay truly make you feel more successful?

When you seize an opportunity to start your own business and take charge of your career, you have the ability to carve out the perfect future for yourself.

As you consider your options, such as starting a new, independent business, buying an existing business or a franchise that comes with a track record of success and its own operating manual, ask yourself what you mean by success.

Rank these qualities of success in order of importance for you.

Start by defining your idea of success. Is it:

- Getting rich?
- Having enough money to travel or retire comfortably?
- Having a job that you love?
- The ability to send your children to college
- Having the time to give back to your community, whether that means volunteering at your local food pantry or serving on a nonprofit board?
- Having a spiritual life, full of exploration and learning?
- Combining the goals of your life and your career, which may mean working in health care or education?
- Contributing to a goal larger than yourself, such as helping to make the world a better place?
- Feeling greater self-worth?
- Controlling your own future?
- Getting the flexibility, you need to create all of the above?
- Balancing work and life?

You may want to add a few of your own priorities to personalize your journey:

_____

_____

_____

Once you decide exactly what you want, your search for a business will be that much easier because you will know more about the life you desire.

TWO

The Upside of Starting Your Own Business

Maybe you're bored or have accomplished everything you set out to do with your first career. Or maybe you've been laid off or downsized or are just looking for a change in an uncertain economy. Entrepreneurship may be just what you need to craft your dream career. And whether due to the midlife doldrums or a career that has recently let you down, lots of folks see starting a business as a way to find new meaning in their work.

About 35 percent of all new businesses were started by people over the age of 50, according to a recent study.* The midlife entrepreneur was even the subject of a US Senate hearing titled, "In Search of a Second Act: The Challenges and Advantages of Senior Entrepreneurship."

According to testimony before the committee, entrepreneurs between the ages of 55 and 64 are starting businesses at a faster rate than people in their 20s and 30s.

But the news is hardly surprising since everyone knows 60 is the new 40, and extensive life and business experience can pay big dividends in business.

Midlife is the Perfect Time to Start a New Business

Not only are those over 50 more likely to start a business, they also bring to the table years of acquired knowledge and wisdom gained through decades of coping with wins and losses in life and career, which helps them succeed in this new venture.

Midlife career changers are also more likely to have gained the financial wherewithal to get to the next level either by buying a business or a franchise. Many folks have successfully tapped into their retirement savings to finance a whole new career with a more reliable long-term stream of income. As we have all learned by the age of 50, almost every job comes with a sell-by date. If you haven't moved up to the next level in a while, there's a good chance the job won't last.

Franchising is Way More Then Fast Food or Retail

In fact, there are lots of franchise opportunities in service businesses. In these you can find ways to make a real difference in people's lives and use the skills you developed in your first career.

The International Franchise Association projects business, commercial, and residential services to be among the fastest growing sectors in franchising. If you're interested in helping people get control over an aspect of their personal or professional lives, there may be no better time to start your next career.

The advantage of a franchise is that it offers time-tested systems, plus training and ongoing support. And while the world of franchising is huge—80+ industries are represented—and can seem daunting, a franchise coach can help you get started with your research.

Opportunities I like in the growing service sector include:

- Senior Care
- Health and Wellness
- Home Maintenance and Repair
- Disaster Recovery
- Pet Services
- Business Services

You will find more information about these sectors in Part Two, Chapter Four.

Whichever business you choose to enter, topmost in your mind should be your specific personal goals, whether that's more control over your career or maximizing earnings. Either way, you can find what you're looking for in the world of franchising.

Earn the Really Big Bucks

While your own individual markers for success may have little to do with the size of your paycheck, the fact is most people who earn the really big bucks do it by becoming entrepreneurs.

You're far more likely to become a millionaire by owning your own business than any other method. But, as we all learn sooner or later, it's not only about the money. It's also about finding fulfillment in your work, feeling appreciated for what you do and controlling your own destiny.

As we mentioned earlier, according to *The Millionaire Next Door*, 70 percent of American millionaires earned their wealth by owning their own business.

Get a Jump on the Next Great Wave of Layoffs

This seems to be an era of big mergers, operations improvements, and outsourcing. Upbeat PR announcements of these are usually accompanied by words like streamlining, efficiencies, and synergies. We've all learned that these terms mean mass layoffs. And there always seems to be another round coming.

First, we hear about the economies of scale and efficiencies to be generated. Step two quickly follows, when a fresh group of experienced professionals are cut loose from the workforce, in too many cases, due to the age discrimination world we live in. They may find themselves adrift and without prospects. While the company casually sails along, these good employees, sloughed off to reduce payroll costs, may find themselves with reduced prospects.

For working folks between the ages of 45 and retirement, anecdotal evidence abounds about how difficult it is to get a new job with a strong future, even at a time of increased awareness of age discrimination.

But these talented professionals are hardly without options.

One possibility is to consider putting your skills and experience to work for yourself in a business of your own.

STORY FROM THE FIELD

When a Layoff Spurs a Search for Something More

If, like Don Ballantine, you're over the age of 50 when you get your pink slip, even if your prospects for a new job are good, you will likely enter a serious period of soul-searching. Not only may you face age discrimination in your job search, but you also may have entered a different phase in your life, where you are re-examining your goals and life choices. You find yourself wondering: Is it time to rethink your work-life balance? Maybe you decide you want to prioritize enjoying your work or, possibly, work fewer hours.

For Ballantine, the choice was complicated by the economic crisis that followed the market crash and housing bust of 2008. Laid off, even after the economy was picking up, he decided a moment of introspection was overdue.

After more than 30 years as a mechanical engineer, his division's largest customer, a military contractor, pulled its business from his employer. At the age of 51, Ballantine was cut loose with a six-month severance package. He took advantage of the classes his company made available to him to help him figure out his next stage. One of those classes introduced him to the option of a franchise.

Before long, Ballantine lined up another job doing exactly what he had been doing for three decades. But doubts started creeping into his mind. "I thought, is this it?" Ballantine recounted. After thinking it through, he concluded: "The hell with it. I'll take a chance on myself for once instead of doing what I've been doing until I die. Maybe I can do something different."

He had a couple of friends with franchises, and he thought if they could succeed, then he could, too. With the help of a franchise coach, he started doing his research. After looking at a series of franchises, he found himself drawn to one. Not only was he attracted to the work for personal reasons, he was impressed with their business model.

"One system really grabbed me," he said, referring to a franchise company that helps people with disabilities stay in their homes. "I could help people instead of making bombs to blow them up." Plus, he liked the company.

"I was very impressed by their marketing strategy, and their people seemed to really like what they were doing," he said.

Since two of his own family members had disabilities as a result of complications from diabetes, Ballantine felt a personal connection to the mission of helping people deal with their mobility issues around the house. His ability to empathize with people who were facing the difficulty of adjusting to life with a new disability helped him create lasting connections that were also good for business.

While Ballantine was confident about his mechanical abilities—"I can put anything together"—when it came to the other aspects of running a business, from bookkeeping to managing payroll and benefits, he felt less sure of himself.

"That's where the franchise company's support really came in handy. The franchise is fanatical about opening steps," he said. "There are biweekly meetings with people in corporate" where they discuss everything from finding a location and negotiating a lease to paying taxes.

"They support you every step of the way," he said. "I wouldn't have been able to open without learning what I learned from them."

As part of the preparation process, he talked to franchisees, some of whom were more helpful than others, but he finds the idea of sharing one's experiences with fellow franchisees one of the most compelling aspects of having a franchise.

"Talk to a Franchise"

Ballantine particularly likes the franchise's program, "Talk to a Franchise," where an existing franchisee talks to three or four potential franchisees on a conference call, and they get the opportunity to ask whatever questions come to mind.

"I'm really blunt with them," he said. For starters, he tells them that starting a franchise like his is a lot of work.

After four years with his new business, while he acknowledged making some mistakes along the way, he said he would definitely do it again.

One of the advantages he most appreciates is achieving total control of his life. And while he may sometimes have to work late, if the ocean sparkles particularly brightly one day, he knows he can take an hour for a swim if he feels like it.

"Not a bad way to make a living. Not bad at all."

You Can Successfully Manage Risk

Any challenging endeavor, like hiking the Pacific Crest Trail, rafting down the Colorado River or starting your own business, offers the thrill of success. And just like you wouldn't start a 30-day hike without preparation, you shouldn't start a business without first doing your research.

The biggest stumbling block for many would-be career changers is fear: fear of change, fear of risk, fear of the unknown. The more you know, the more you can lower your risk. If the prospect of a steep learning curve sounds intimidating, think of it as preparation. Just remember the old saying that luck is what happens when preparation meets opportunity.

Good preparation can turn the odds in your favor. You should know as much as you can before laying any of your money on the line. As we've discussed, the way to get the most information about your future business is with a franchise. And a good franchise coach can help match you with the franchise that is right for you.

Reinvent Yourself for a New Career

As we all know, most of us will reach a time in our careers when we have to reinvent ourselves for an evolving economy. Some of us remain with the same employer but with a different job title. Some go back to school, while others start new businesses.

First, stop thinking of yourself as just a job title, whether your field is in finance, marketing, human resources, technology, or whatever.

No matter how you've spent your early career, we all end up developing a specific expertise. When you run your own business, you need to learn about every aspect of the business, from managing staff to operations. Rather than sounding intimidating, such a task allows you to tap all your talents developed over a lifetime of experiences.

If there are some aspects of the business that you are completely uninterested in doing, you'll want to find out in advance if those are tasks that can be delegated to others. If not, you're probably looking at a business that is not a good match for you.

Ready for a New Adventure, Not Retirement

Maybe you've reached the stage where you've met all your major financial responsibilities, you've put some rainy-day funds aside, and you're ready to create success for yourself, instead of your corporate employer. What better time than right now to test those creative ideas you've been mulling over for years?

When you have a road map to help show you the way, you're not just flying by the seat of your pants, you're using your smarts to prepare a plan that will maximize your chances for success.

These days when people enter their 40s or 50s and start planning for retirement, increasingly, this means instead of exiting the workforce, they are getting ready for the next stage of a career.

Contrary to most people's preconceptions, the most active group of entrepreneurs in the country are folks in midlife, ages 45 to 64, not the young techies from Silicon

Valley. According to one study, "Older workers…have consistently exceeded younger workers in entrepreneurial activity."*

In fact, retirement is seen by many as a way to transition into a new line of work altogether. "The top reason 'retire-preneurs' started their own business was to work on their own terms (82%)," the study found.* Almost half of middle-class Americans in their 50s continue working because they don't think they've saved enough to retire, according to a Harris Poll.* More than half of baby boomers expect to work at least to the age of 66 or older, and ⅔ expect to work for pay in retirement, according to Gallup polls.* Many in midlife, examining their priorities and hopes for the future, find a franchise can help them take control of their careers. A franchise can also help them achieve the lives they always wanted but were unable to obtain in a regular workaday job.

If you're like many Americans, your work-time horizon is much longer than it used to be. As a result, there's less reason than ever to stick it out with a dead-end job or sink into despair after being downsized out of a job.

Surveys show that most of us don't have enough retirement savings, and we can't really retire the way our parents or grandparents did because we're living longer and require more money to make it. Many don't even want to fully retire.

STORY FROM THE FIELD

An Alternative to Retirement

Edward Flanagan, of Huntington Valley, PA, started a new franchise at the age of 53, and he said he enjoys his business so much that he intends to work "until I die."

After Flanagan had risen to chief financial officer for a real-estate developer, the industry started collapsing with the 2008 market crash, and Flanagan began to look for new opportunities. He hoped to parlay his financial experience into a new career that he could control.

After we met and started talking about various opportunities in franchising, he decided he liked the upside of purchasing a franchise, from a ready-to-go system already in place to a network of support that would help him get through the start-up phase.

A couple weeks later, he went to a Franchise Discovery Day at **Expense Reduction Analysts** and decided to take the leap.

Now, a decade later, he couldn't be happier with his new business, in which he helps his clients find cost savings, which translate into a fatter bottom line for their businesses. He takes personal pride in the fact that with the help of a network of analysts, his fellow franchisees, Flanagan is able to obtain an average savings of 20 percent for his clients.

In his new career, he's achieved increased income with the potential to earn even more and far more freedom to allow him the lifestyle he desires.

While he achieved what he hoped for, Flanagan acknowledged the transition wasn't exactly easy. For one thing, when you own the joint, you carry the load.

> *"When you're your own boss, it's all on you…*
> *You've got to keep plugging away," he noted.*

At the time of his purchase, the US economy was still struggling to recover from a crippling recession, and many business owners were loath to think outside the box, even for a service that Flanagan viewed as a no-brainer opportunity to make the difference between profit and loss for many businesses.

While Flanagan acknowledged the hard work he faced as a startup, his business is now rolling along quite well, growing by 20 percent each year.

"The best thing is getting referrals," he said. But that takes time, through making contacts and establishing networks and business relationships. Now more than 70 percent of his clients result from referrals.

The best advice Flanagan offered for those about to embark on a new career as owners of their own businesses:

> *"You've got to stick with it…*
> *If you're willing to follow a successful franchise model,*
> *you can really have a nice lifestyle and make good money."*

Of course, not all business types travel the same trajectory, but the point is to be prepared for a few belly flops on your way to scoring.

As Flanagan emphasizes, the rewards are worth sticking to the plan.

Whatever You Decide—Don't Sell Yourself Short!

Instead of thinking of yourself as a set of skills defined by job titles or direct experience in a particular industry, separate out the activities you performed in various roles you've taken on in your life. Inventory your skills to get a truly accurate read on your experience. The key is to keep your mind open to possibilities you may never before have considered.

For example, a plant manager increasingly frustrated at work feared his skills managing a large manufacturing plant with a unionized work force would not easily transfer to franchise ownership. But as he began his research, he realized his experience meeting deadlines, working on tight budgets, and motivating employees sometimes resistant to instructions, would serve him well in other businesses. He eventually opened a temp staffing franchise and has been enjoying his new profitable career for more than five years.

Likewise, the first decades of my own career would seem to have nothing to do with senior care, the industry I chose for my first franchise. But skills built in one type of business can transfer well to another. By the time I turned 50, I had experience creating local awareness of a business, providing excellent customer service and developing strong referral relationships—exactly the skills I would need in senior care, which is why I felt confident making the shift from finance to senior care.

Remember, when it comes to franchises, the companies provide extensive training and support to help you transfer your skills to a new business. What you want to have are the skills necessary for the new business. That combination will enable you to rise above the competition.

Not Ready to Quit Your Day Job?

Starting a franchise can be an attractive option for people who have always wanted to have their own business but may not be ready to quit their day jobs just yet.

Being able to profit directly from your labor, increase your independence, and gain better control over the future of your career can be compelling incentives to start looking for your next career move.

One good option for those not yet willing to leave their jobs is a category of franchise called semi-absentee, in which the owner hires a manager to manage the day-to-day aspects of the business while the owner manages the manager. This way the owner only needs to work part-time. A whole range of opportunities exist in this category. You can keep your job while you plan either a whole new career or the "retire-preneur" phase of your life.

STORY FROM THE FIELD

A Franchise Can be an On-Ramp to Your Next Career

John Baldino of Milford, Delaware found himself looking for his next career move but was not yet ready to leave his corporate job. He liked the idea of being in business for himself for all the usual reasons:

> *He could keep all the profits that flowed from his labor,*
> *increase his independence,*
> *and gain better control over his future.*

He and his wife Kathleen, also with a corporate background, started researching semi-absentee franchises, a business model in which you manage the manager you hire to run the business. The manage-the-manager model allows the owner to work only part-time on the business.

The franchise that rose to the top of their list was a hair salon. In this franchise, the owner's role is defined as the people manager and cheerleader. The owner's responsibility is to check the numbers and be involved in recruiting, training and marketing, plus scoping out the next business location, since the average franchisee eventually owns five units. When you consider the typical outlet generates cash flow of $85,000 per year, this clearly is an opportunity for big earnings.

After starting his investigation, Baldino said they went through months of evaluation—a type of mutual vetting period—before they signed the contract.

> *"The process of*
> *how to run this business is very well defined…*
> *There was a clear understanding of what*
> *it takes to be successful."*

Baldino particularly liked how the company's procedures and technology all worked together.

For example, this franchisor offers its owners an iPad app, through which franchisees can get real-time data about their salon business.

Owners can actually watch the salon's activity from wherever they are. They can see which stylists are currently cutting hair and which may be on a break.

Many of this company's franchisees come from corporate America, and the quality they tend to share is an interest in conservative growth. They want their own businesses but don't want a lot of risk, so they prefer to start slow. Usually they keep their corporate job for at least the first two years.

Over time, franchisees are encouraged to purchase additional salons because a multi-unit operation offers economies of scale, as well as greater management flexibility. For example, managers can shift stylists around to different stores to meet demand.

The Baldinos started with one franchise location, opened their second a year later and two years later had their third.

"I have a great general manager. She runs the salons," he said. "I just have to mix in the right people."

Baladino estimates he puts in about ten hours a week and his wife adds some hours of her own. Since their managers handle the nitty-gritty of the day-to-day operations, he and his wife can think about the bigger picture, such as marketing and growing their business.

While Baladino isn't ready to leave his corporate job, he can imagine the day he will transition completely to small-business owner. By then, it may not be such a small business. As for now, they're looking at one location at a time.

Starting with a small operation that offers future growth has great appeal, especially for folks who may be anxious about venturing out on their own.

*A semi-absentee franchise system like the Baldinos chose
can help ease the transition.*

Control Your Destiny

There's no better time than now to try something you've always dreamt about—that is, to research ways to take charge of your career, to see if you can find a way to become your own boss. Instead of just a job, your 9-to-5 can become as fun and stimulating as any other part of your life.

Notice we don't say, "Now is the time to start your own business." That's because you might complete your research and decide you don't want to own a business, after all. That's OK. When you start your research, you simply will not know what answers you'll find. The key is to learn as much as you can, so you can then make an informed decision.

Opportunities abound. The first thing you have to do is to overcome the inertia that keeps you in the corporate world. Then start exploring ways you can escape the humdrum of fulfilling someone else's career goals

As the highly respected business coach Jim Rohn eloquently pointed out,

*"If you don't design your own life plan,
you'll fall into somebody else's plan.
And guess what they have planned for you?
Not much."*

If you experienced a sudden tightening in your gut at even the thought of becoming an entrepreneur, remember you risk absolutely nothing by conducting an exploration.

While everyone has risk-averse voices whispering in their ears, you can quiet those fears through solid research. When you deepen your knowledge by understanding the actual facts, you can make a more informed choice. As we emphasize, you'll find that in many ways owning your own business can be less risky than remaining an employee in today's revolving-door economy.

Don't worry if you don't have a background in your new business. A franchise can help you attain your second career in an entirely new arena. With a franchise you get to operate your own business while having a team of experts behind you. You get a tried-and-true business model and marketing expertise, as well as training and ongoing support. In short, you break out of the gate with a head start.

THREE

How Do I Know If I have What it Takes?

The only way to answer that question is to look inside yourself. We propose an in-depth approach to help you conduct your own self-assessment. And if you choose to work with a franchise coach, you may be asked to do a professional assessment as well.

The assessment we use helps us to understand your professional side at a deeper level, so we can find a franchise that is a great match for you. That way, you know you will be in a business where you can best take advantage of your strengths. Likewise, you will avoid businesses you may not be well suited for.

If you do not use a franchise coach, we recommend you start by reviewing the details that fill up a typical resumé, starting with your educational background.

Your Experience & Background

Keep in mind that buying a franchise is a great way to reinvent your career. Don't merely recall the aspects of your education that you've put to use so far in your career. A franchise, with all its expertise and training, can help you break free of past constraints. You will learn how to apply your skills to new tasks and start doing work you enjoy. Your natural strengths or educational background can help your learning curve.

The key is to avoid making assumptions about what you're good at, based on your career so far. Create a list of your strengths, based on career, academic and life experiences. What did you study in school? What have you always enjoyed doing? Hobbies, interests, etc.

Are you strong in science, math, or do you excel in communicating? Don't worry if this list doesn't include any specific business topics. Study of the humanities offers great insights into human nature, which is a strength in running a business. More obviously, being strong in science and math prepares you well for businesses that require technical knowledge or a sense for numbers. If you're willing to learn, you can gain great benefits from good training and be prepared to excel in business.

What do you like to do in your free time? Maybe you prefer more solitary activities, like crafts and reading. Or perhaps you gravitate towards more social activities. If you pursue a business that allows you to spend your time on the tasks you enjoy, you'll likely be more motivated to do what you need to succeed.

Career Experience

Make a list of the different skills you've gained over the years in your career. Stick with specifics. Start with activities and then link the skills associated with them, so you don't inadvertently dismiss certain skills you may not realize you've gained.

For example, if you worked in marketing, you likely developed lead strategies, networked though local organizations or trade groups, compiled marketing materials, cultivated regular customers, tailored your efforts to suit clients' particular needs and established ongoing relationships along the way. These activities entail skills in communications, organization and marketing, to name just a few.

Once you've reviewed your career and education, we recommend you undertake two types of self-assessment on your own. First, you want to figure out if you're cut out to be a business owner. You need to consider your greatest attributes in the workplace and figure out what you would be prepared to learn.

An Entrepreneur's Checklist

Running your own business generally requires certain qualities or character traits, though you need not possess every one before you make the decision to create a new career for yourself. As in most adventures in life, you can prepare to become what you seek to be. Not everyone who completes a marathon is a natural runner. You can train your mind as well as your body. Knowing where to start is the first step.

Consider the following qualities. Ask yourself if you have:

Sufficient Drive

Are you committed to your new business idea enough to see yourself doing it in six months, next year, in five years? This is something to seriously consider before embarking on all the preparation and research necessary to enable you to become successful. Do you have the energy to work hard, especially at the beginning, as you learn the system?

Faith in Your Ability to Make Things Happen

Belief in yourself and your vision may be the single most important thing that keeps you going when you reach an obstacle.

Independence

Have you always been a self-starter? No one will be on your case to make a deadline or even get to work on time. Being the boss requires you to be comfortable making decisions, which means you have to take the time to really know your stuff. If this makes you uncomfortable, then entrepreneurship may not be for you.

If, on the other hand, you would be willing to focus on your business if your effort directly impacted your income, starting your own business may be worth further exploration.

Emotional Resilience to Bounce Back from Temporary Setbacks
If losing a key employee will send you reeling, rather than doubling down to learn what happened so you can improve, you might want to reconsider leaving the corporate world.

Comfort with Uncertainty
Are you comfortable putting your money behind your ideas? While lots of resources exist to help you finance your new business, you certainly want sufficient capital to get you through the start-up phase—usually at least $50,000. In addition, since it will take time before your new business starts to earn profits, you need to be comfortable with uncertainty. Here's where that faith in yourself really comes in handy.

The Ability to Reassess & Reinvent
When something's not working, you may have to figure out a new way to operate, whether it comes to your resources, operations or your profits. If you're one who likes to stick to the tried and true, a franchise may be a good option since the franchise company will be constantly reviewing its systems to optimize results.

Willingness to Follow a System
If you can accept following an established, proven plan, a franchise may be your perfect choice. If you prefer, however, to solve every puzzle yourself, an independent business may be a better option.

Most Importantly: Do You Have Your Family's Support?
A good conversation upfront about what starting a new business entails, including more responsibility than you might be used to, as well as capital investment, can go a long way toward assuaging anxiety.

How Long Will It Take Your New Business to Reach Profitability?
Some business types have a longer start-up phase before the business starts to generate income. You need to research these numbers ahead of time to ensure you are adequately capitalizing your business.

This spotlights a key strength of investing in a franchise model. Since you are able to speak to franchisees who have started the exact same type of business, you have a better chance of pinpointing the true investment amount.

A realistic appraisal will prepare you for success far better than wishful thinking

The assessment marks only the beginning of your journey, as it gives you enough data to start a conversation with a franchise coach. The coach will take you through a process, which will help you understand if you're right for business ownership. You will still need to investigate the types of businesses for which you might be best suited.

Assess Your Skills

Next you will undertake an analysis of your skills, answering the question: What skills do I possess? With the right prompts, you'll likely find that your decade or three in the workforce, plus your life experience, have given you more entrepreneurial skills than you realize

To accurately gauge your preparedness for any new endeavor, you should consider all the skills you have accumulated that can be transferred to a new career. As you take an inventory of your skills, you want to dive deep into the details of your day, both now and in prior positions, to accurately assess your strengths and transferable skills.

Take a Personal Inventory

1. List what you do in an average workday.
Make a list of all the activities you perform in any given day over a week, since not everything you do happens daily. And don't skip anything you may consider "a no-brainer" or insignificant, because these little things can add up to a very significant skill. If you sometimes have to field phone calls from disgruntled clients, and you've discovered you're really good at calming people's nerves, that's a valuable skill. Even if your job title is IT Manager.

2. Realistically assess your personal strengths.
You don't need to be good at everything, but if recruiting and training employees is an essential aspect of the business, you need to know you can do this day in and day out. Consider core skills such as communications, business acumen, managing people, marketing, etc. Be honest with yourself and stay clear of businesses that require reliance on skills that are not among your strengths.

3. Are you detail-oriented or more the big-picture thinker?
If you're a numbers person, you may want to find a business that can capitalize on this valuable skill. Or maybe you prefer developing strategies that can make the whole operation run more smoothly.

4. Do you have good follow-through?
Building a clientele involves not only making good connections but following through to convert these new contacts into lasting relationships. Follow-through can also be an essential attribute in managing staff.

5. Are you a people person?
Do you love being around and meeting new people? Do you strike up conversations easily and enjoy learning about other people's interests and goals? Many businesses require a whole range of people skills in hiring and managing staff and attracting and keeping customers, but there are lots of businesses where the owner has a less outgoing role.

Personal inventory in hand, you're now ready to begin researching businesses that would best match your skills. As you start looking for businesses that might suit your particular set of strengths and skills, you may need to do a periodic gut check. Questions to ask yourself:

Do Your Skills Match Your Business of Choice?
Use the inventory of your skills to see if they match those necessary for your chosen business type. Don't worry if they don't line up exactly, but you require an honest appraisal to make an honest assessment.

Clients have often told me that a key benefit of talking to existing franchise owners is the ability to determine the skills necessary for success in this business. After all, nobody knows what the most important skills are better than somebody who is already running the same kind of business.

One way to think about this is to consider: If you were offered a job running a business similar to the franchise under consideration, would you feel you have the skills to run that business successfully? If you answered yes, but you hesitate to accept a similar role for your own business, the difference is probably just nerves and not indicative of your likelihood of success.

This goes back to the idea of not selling yourself short. Some people may find that the thought of operating their own business gives them butterflies similar to stage fright, but if you've done your preparation, you will have everything you need to succeed.

Take your personal interests into account!
Your interests are highly important, since you don't want to choose a business that requires you to spend your days in activities you don't like. Pay particular attention to how well your interests fit the type of tasks you will be working on. This will be more significant than the type of service the business provides.

The whole point is to make a change in which you can find greater income, along with freedom and personal fulfillment.

Business Skills to Consider as You Undertake Your Inventory

- **Leadership** – do you have the ability to recruit, motivate, and retain good employees?
- **Management** – which includes abilities to assess and develop employees
- **Organization** – planning, scheduling, assigning, and delegating
- **Marketing**
- **Selling**
- **Communication** – writing, explaining, listening, interpreting
- **Creativity**
- **Self-Education** – the ability to educate yourself
- **Public speaking**
- **Leading Meetings**

- **Critical Thinking** – including problem solving & decision-making
- **Negotiation**

As you read about specific ideas to research, keep in mind your personal goals and strengths to help you make the smartest choice possible. See Appendix III for a handy worksheet to help you compile your attributes. Creating a career to enhance your personal and professional growth should be a journey you can enjoy every step of the way. After all, taking positive action toward a better future should be enough to bring a smile to your face. Enjoy the process!

PART TWO

ad·van·tage
(noun)

A condition or circumstance
that puts one in a favorable or superior position

synonyms:

upper hand
edge
lead

The opportunity to gain something; benefit or profit.

synonyms:

benefit
profit
gain
good
interest
welfare
well-being
enjoyment
satisfaction
comfort
ease
convenience

FOUR

Why a Franchise Could Be Your Ticket

As we have seen, going into business for yourself can offer a fantastic path forward, not only as a way to reinvigorate your career and increase your earnings, but also to gain new satisfaction from your life. While it may sound trite, you really can achieve the dream of turning your job into the life you always wanted.

One of the best ways to get to that goal is to buy into a great franchise operation. A franchise can significantly shorten your learning curve when starting a new business. In addition, if you are thorough in your research, your chance for success goes way up with a franchise. It's all about knowing how to leverage the value from a franchise. You gain a well-run operation, already humming with many profitable outlets, which helps you maximize the upward trajectory of your business and, of course, your earnings.

With a great franchise, you can access the collective experiences of many successful business owners who over the years have helped perfect the franchise operating system, their blueprint for success.

The beauty of the system is that it's all laid out for you. You follow the franchisor's guidelines on exactly how to operate the business—everything from how to set up your shop to how much money you should have on hand to last through the initial start-up phase. The system also includes the strategic positioning of the brand and marketing expertise. This reflects years of operating multiple units owned by franchisees or, in some cases, by the franchisor as well.

Compared to launching your own independent startup, which requires you to invent all your own systems and continually adjust to changing market forces all on your own, when you buy a franchise, your business gets a complete program and a team of experts assisting you on day one. This includes everything you need to successfully operate your business, such as time-saving software and a network of suppliers. As you learn the system, a good franchise will offer training and ongoing support to get you across the finish line.

As with everything in life, there are no guarantees, but if you do your research and select a franchise that matches your skills and interests, you have a far greater chance of success than with almost any other type of new business. A franchise is the only way I know to start a business where you get the opportunity to learn all you need to know in advance.

In this section, you will find lots of helpful tips on choosing a business in which you can best succeed, as well as strategies to help you understand what you must do as a franchisee to achieve your goals. It's important to understand that the most successful franchisees understand the business as a type of partnership, where both the franchisor and the franchisee are equally important to success.

For most franchise purchasers, the idea of getting a complete business in a beautifully wrapped package is the main attraction.

Franchising Offers a Diverse Array of Business Types

From consulting to construction, tutoring to senior care, and haircuts to weight-loss centers—to list just the tip of the iceberg—franchising offers a career to suit nearly everyone's interests and expertise.

Delve Into the Possibilities

Look around and notice the array of business types and services that have popped up to serve the evolving needs of our economy. What do you wish you were doing with your days? There's probably a franchise for you. Check out the International Franchise Association at www.franchise.org where you can view lists of franchise types, as well as other resources. We included a list of franchise types in the appendix.

Lack Experience in Your Preferred Business? A Franchise Can Fill in the Gaps

Most entrepreneurs who buy a franchise have no experience in their new industry. With a strong franchise, this should not be a problem. The new franchisees can feel comfortable knowing the training that comes with their franchise will help them build successful businesses, outperforming even established independent competitors.

When you pay a franchisor a start-up fee, which usually ranges from $40,000 to $70,000, you get proven systems and training to get your business to profitability.

In our current economic environment, little mom-and-pops often find it tough to compete. A proven business model, which often comes with a coordinated advertising campaign, offers great benefits that can mean the difference between success and failure. You can start your own business with a franchise and still have lots of the same perks as an independent business owner, plus many advantages they don't have.

A Great Option to Reinvigorate Your Career

Instead of facing another dead-end at a faceless corporation, midlife career change can lead you to more opportunity for growth through entrepreneurship. With the business services category so strong in recent years, a franchise might be just the ticket to help you transition from corporate life to operating a business of your own.

Economic indicators continue to be strong in the franchise sector of the economy. The growth in the number of franchised business services—which includes executive coaching, employment services, workplace drug testing, and IT services—has continued to outpace most other franchise sectors.

STORY FROM THE FIELD

Escape Office Politics & Shorten Your Learning Curve

Mirroring the desires of many MBAs of his generation, Bob Riesenbach always dreamed of starting his own business. After twenty-three years working for big corporations, he started investigating his options.

"I was tired of bureaucracy and politics," explained Riesenbach, who has an MBA from the Wharton School of the University of Pennsylvania and 20-plus years of corporate experience. He first started looking at businesses for sale but didn't find much in his geographic area "beyond pizza joints and bars."

He soon decided a franchise made the most sense. "I didn't want to start from scratch, and I thought I could learn from other people's experiences," he said.

After we met at a Philadelphia area networking meeting, Riesenbach started looking closely at several franchise possibilities, eventually choosing to buy a franchise that took the most advantage of the skills he had spent his career acquiring.

Before long, he left his marketing position at a large chain of convenience stores and ventured out on his own. As he recalls, he was ready to leave behind corporate America to forge his own path building a business of his own.

Is there a catch?
Not when you love what you do
and know it's all for you!

Riesenbach has built his new business, CMIT Solutions of Cherry Hill, New Jersey, a provider of information technology services for small and mid-sized businesses, with the support of a strong network of fellow franchisees.

"The strength of the organization comes from our partnership with other owners," Riesenbach explained. The franchise company sets up formal networking groups, and Riesenbach is able to speak regularly to his fellow owners at least once a week.

The franchise came with lots of other advantages, as well, including fully vetted resources, such as vendors and marketing services, plus annual conventions that provide him an opportunity to share best practices and lessons from the field with his fellow franchisees. With CMIT Solutions, franchisees have the ability to leverage the size of their network. They provide clients with discounted prices on services from vendors, such as Dell or Microsoft, that would likely not be available to a small independent business.

Besides enjoying the benefits from the franchisee network, Riesenbach gains great satisfaction from being in charge of his own business and eliminating the red tape of a corporate hierarchy.

> *"I love having my own company," he said.*
> *"Here I can make my own decisions."*

Riesenbach's company continues to grow and has been honored by Philadelphia Business Journal as one of its Top IT Pros. He was also honored by his franchisor as Rookie of the Year in 2012 and Franchisee of the Year for 2015, excelling in criteria that included exceptional customer service, total revenue, revenue increase, operations, and number of managed clients.

Sometimes a prospective franchisee will ask whether he might have saved the cost of a franchise and just built this business on his own—after all, he already had so much relevant experience. Riesenbach counters that he thinks the value he got from the franchise vastly exceeds the cost.

> *"When people say why not just do it on your own,*
> *so you don't have to pay royalties, ignore those people,"*
> *Riesenbach advised.*
> *"I feel I'm getting a lot more value than I'm paying for."*

Riesenbach's Top Tips for Prospective Franchisees:

Talk to a lot of existing franchise owners, whose contact information can be found in the (FDD) Franchise Disclosure Document. He looked seriously at three or four franchises to start. Research helped him choose the one that turned out to be the best fit.

Have realistic expectations. Know it takes a while to get a new business going.

Be prepared to work hard.

Look for a good match with your skills and interests.

What You Get with a Franchise

A Strong Record of Success

The franchisees I've worked with have had a 96 percent success rate. The key to their success begins with research, research, research. They followed our process to figure out which franchise was right for them and which franchises offered the best chance of success.

A Well-Documented Track Record and Built-in Networking
Franchises have the advantage of experience from their dozens, hundreds, or thousands of franchisees around the country. These folks, who have walked the same path you're setting forth on, can provide you with much valuable information to help you succeed. This network of fellow franchisees can offer great tips to help you deal with most issues that arise. Many franchise companies have formal systems that enable franchisees to share best practices on a regular basis. Most franchisees I have worked with find this network an invaluable benefit of a franchise business.

Backroom Expertise
You get expert marketing and support from the franchise as well as expertise on how to build your business as dozens have done before you. The franchise company can be an invaluable partner if you hit obstacles along the way. Their experts can help you brainstorm ways to progress and succeed.

Readily Available Information
Nearly every detail you would want to learn about a franchise before getting into it is easy to find. You can discover details about the finances of a franchise, the background of its executives, franchise fees and the other costs of buying the franchise, the franchisee's obligations, as well as a full list of franchisees in the Franchise Disclosure Document (FDD). Franchisors are required to disclose this material to prospective franchisees. About a third of franchisors even provide information about financial performance (Item 19 in the FDD). Interviews with franchisees offer a great way to verify any information you get from the franchisor.

All these advantages of a franchise are what enable you to select one that will maximize your earning potential and simultaneously minimize your risk.

How? Because with a franchise
you can find out everything you need to
know to succeed – again, BEFORE you have to make any investment.

FIVE

The Right Strategy For the Right Franchise

As we emphasize, there is no such thing as the perfect franchise. Since franchises come in all sizes and shapes, the goal is to make the perfect match: Choose the right franchise for you. And, frankly, not every franchise is suitable for everyone.

One of the most important aspects of this search is to start with the right frame of mind. First, throw out all your preconceived notions about the type of business you always dreamed of operating, or the one your mother/father/best friend said would be perfect for you.

Your best tool is a fresh set of eyes. The truth is, you can never tell what type of business will end up rising to the top after a thorough research process.

Sometimes listening to your research is easier said than done. My own experience selecting my first franchise provides a perfect case in point.

When I started exploring a senior care franchise, one of the first questions I sought to answer was: How many local competitors are there? In my region, I found about seventy senior care businesses. I immediately concluded that seventy was far too many, the market was too crowded for another company, and I should check out a different business sector. Fortunately, I realized I was merely making an assumption. I gave myself the advice I often give to my clients: Test that assumption. Was the market really too crowded?

I did my research, which showed there actually was room in the market. When I completed my research, I moved forward and invested in a senior care franchise. Buying that franchise was probably the best business decision I've ever made. If I had not decided to test my assumptions, I would have passed right by that excellent opportunity,

I have laid out some pointers that will help you make the most of your time as you begin your research. Before you begin, you might want to review the work you completed at the end of Part I. Keep in mind your unique portfolio of skills as you read.

The Way to Select the Right Franchise for You

Evaluate the Role of the Owner

During your research on the ins and outs of the franchise system, pay particular attention to the role of the owner in operating the business. This means the types of tasks you would spend the bulk of your days doing. Some owners spend much of their time building clientele, while others manage employees or operations. You should have a clear understanding of what the franchise company expects owners to do to maximize success. Not only do you want to ensure your skills and experience match this job, but you want to make sure it's a job you want.

Separate Your Business Decision from Your Passion

When it comes to running a business, your main job will be *managing* the business, no matter what product or service you're selling. Consequently, what should concern you most is the day-to-day work required to succeed, not the type of business. You want your decision to be driven first and foremost by how much you want to take on the role the owner has in this business.

The role of the owner is as important as the tasks of the business. Just because you love cooking doesn't mean you want to jump into the restaurant business. After all, most restaurant owners aren't in the kitchen. They're managing the front of the room, greeting customers and supervising staff. Consequently, this job often requires the owner to be a people person and effective manager.

Maybe you've been thinking for almost all your adult life about how you might like to open a little bakery or café because you love to bake and would enjoy having all your friends drop by for socializing and coffee. You might want to look more closely at what the owner of the business does. What you'll likely find is that the owner is mainly responsible for managing employees and marketing, focusing on building a customer base to grow revenue.

Generally, the number-one goal of the owner is to build the business, using marketing and advertising. Or the owner might focus on attracting, training and retaining top-notch employees, which allows you to earn a good income, have happy, productive employees and an ever-expanding customer base. This is why your business search should begin by first considering the role of the owner.

You should like—preferably love—what you do day in and day out. But you don't want to limit your choices by linking your selection process to your passion.

This is why it can be a mistake to eliminate businesses that may at first seem less than desirable. Some of these have the capacity to earn you a terrific income—and you may, in fact, love the job of being the owner of that business.

> *The point is
> what owners do can be far different
> from the work of the business.*

A prime example is a home cleaning business, which may not sound appealing if your thoughts immediately center on scrubbing and mopping. But just as many restaurant owners succeed without being culinary geniuses, owners of home cleaning businesses won't be wielding a mop or cleaning toilets.

Owners work on training a stellar crew to do a great job. They spend their time identifying which employees have the capacity to become leaders and managers, and then they groom and develop these people. The owner focuses on the advertising programs that help them acquire a stable of steady clients that will provide repeat business over many years.

The average owner of one great residential cleaning franchise we work with, after establishing his or her business over the first two to three years, achieves annual revenues of more than $1.1 million. The margins are terrific, with the typical owner earning an income of over $240,000 a year. This is just the average owner, not the top franchisees, who obviously do better, sometimes four times the average income.

And while you may have to work lots of hours at the beginning, by about the third year, most owners work only thirty-five hours per week. By then, you've hired a training manager and maybe a quality control manager, and you're managing the managers and focused on marketing and advertising programs, such as direct mail. Turns out, contrary to your first impression, the strengths you need to run a successful cleaning service center more on developing and managing a team.

While a home cleaning business may not sound sexy, what matters is the substance. This is a business that is fairly resistant to economic downturns, tending to do well in both strong and weak economic periods. When it comes to choosing a new business, widening your search. Remain open-minded to businesses that you may have been too quick to cross off your list.

Match the Role of the Owner with Your Skills & Experience

Now that you know the owner's job profile, the question becomes, does this suit you? This is why you need a realistic appraisal of your skills and experience, so you get into a business where you can enjoy your work and apply your talent and skills for long-term success.

Review the inventory of your business skills and dig a little deeper. Don't forget to consider your interests. After all, you want to end up with a business that allows you to enjoy going to work, as well as an opportunity to excel!

Ask yourself, are you proficient in and do you like:

- **Managing people** – Give some thought to the type of employees you prefer. There can be a big difference between managing a white-collar or blue-collar staff.
- **Networking** – Can you connect with people who can help you grow your business?

- **Developing relationships** – Developing repeat clients is all about building relationships. Make sure people know exactly how you will provide excellent service. That way you can earn the trust and confidence of repeat customers.
- **Working with people** – Or do you prefer working on your own?
- **Marketing** – Which might include advertising as well as making presentations?
- **Selling** – This always includes selling yourself, as well as your products or services.
- **Getting into the details** – Or do you prefer to delegate?

When you choose a business, you'll be thinking about the job of the owner and whether that job suits your interests and skills. By all means, be honest with yourself because if you're not, you will be the one who pays the price down the road.

What to Know to Make the Right Selection

What Do You Want, Exactly?
As perhaps the most difficult question of the bunch, you should get a fix on your goals, your constraints and your personal aspirations. You should know how many hours you want to work. Are days or nights preferable? Do you want to work part time? Do you want employees? Do you absolutely hate sales and so know you won't do well in sales? Do you like working with people? Do you want to work at home, or in an office full of people? Do you want a one-person operation, or do you eventually want a chain of shops or offices?

There's a franchise for all of these preferences. Determining what you want will save you a lot of time down the road.

Figure Out if Your Dream Business Measures Up
Still set on opening that little shop around the corner where your friends can always find the bauble of their dreams, or perhaps you have in mind a charming little bed-and-breakfast to be your own vacation paradise? Maybe you've got the TV ideals in mind, like the bar in *Cheers*—"where everybody knows your name"—or the little Vermont inn that Bob Newhart called home for years.

Sounds delightful, but, as we've discussed, running a business is much more than dreams of fun times and quirky customers. Reason must overrule passion. You might be able to find the business that matches your dreams, but I can't emphasize enough that your most important consideration has to be the business of the business. That means figuring out if you have the right skill set to succeed in a particular business.

While it's good to have lots of ideas and a great passion, you don't want to skip the mundane but essential practicalities. If the actual work of the business bores or scares you, instead of getting the little business of your dreams, you may end up with an efficient mechanism for draining your savings.

While you may enjoy the romantic ideal, ask yourself the practical questions so you can determine if this endeavor is really for you.

Five Questions to Help You Get to the Crux of the Numbers and Sense

1. *Do you mind getting to work at 5:30 a.m.?*
    Because when it comes to that little B&B or a coffee shop, that's when business hours begin. Or maybe even earlier. When it comes to the hospitality business, if the customer has a problem, the buck stops with you day or night.

2. *Will the local market generate sufficient earnings?*
    You may think you have the perfect concept to attract folks who didn't know they needed what you have to offer. And maybe you do. But you'll need to know how to generate buzz. Then keep them coming for more. What if you're not a marketing wizard? Then you had better align yourself with a franchise company that is strong in assessing a market and attracting customers.

3. *Have you figured out how much money you need to earn to cover your costs?*
    You need to be prepared with sufficient capital to run your business until you can earn a profit. If the romance—high-end design, fancy Italian espresso machine—in your shop costs more than your earnings can justify, you will have a problem. We highly recommend you consult an accountant to go over whether you have enough to cover your costs to operate.

4. *Will the local labor pool support your needs?*
    Hiring and retaining a good staff is critical. Can you find the workers you need in your area? Does the franchise offer you the tools you need to help you recruit, manage and retain a conscientious, reliable staff?

5. *How many hours are you prepared to work per week to start?*
    Every business requires its own unique schedule from the owner. Make certain you research how many hours the owners work in the franchise you are considering. If you have a lot of other obligations, you may want to reconsider a business with an extremely demanding schedule. You will find plenty of options where you won't have to work more than forty hours per week. It may be even less in the semi-absentee franchise category, which offers opportunities in businesses that require a maximum of ten to twenty hours per week.

Don't Let Lack of Experience Keep You Back

I've met lots of people who fear going into business because they've never done it before, or they don't think they can sell or manage employees. But not all businesses require every skill, and the best thing about a franchise is that it comes with a set of experts to help you learn new skills. What I often tell my clients is "Just because you don't like sales doesn't mean you can't own a business."

That's right. Contrary to popular belief, you can be a successful entrepreneur even if your strength doesn't happen to be cold calling and glad-handing. Opportunities abound with businesses whose customers are drawn in by an effective marketing campaign or a great location. Just think about the shops you notice on your way to work.

Many businesses don't require the owner to be involved with sales. Some large franchise organizations rely on advertising to generate business. In addition, customers may actively seek out a conveniently located operation, often without realizing it's an independently owned franchise. Just to give you a taste, here is a small sample of franchise types that fit these categories:

- Health and wellness
- Pack and ship service
- Lawn care
- House painting
- Maid service
- Home maintenance
- Hair salons
- Academic tutoring
- Pet services

The trick is to make a good match with a franchise that has an established record of working to develop new franchisees into successful members of their team. Working with a franchise coach can help you use your time most efficiently. Let a franchise coach direct you to operations that have the best time-tested systems and a solid track record.

The Success of a Franchise is All About the System

Tweaks to the Model Can Hurt Your Results

A franchise is as good as its system. To get the results touted by the franchise, you must follow their plan.

When franchisees buy into a franchise, they spend weeks if not months learning this system, so they can maximize their results. Still, every year, I come across folks who thought they could make the system work better.

These little "tweaks" usually do more harm than good. If you don't have confidence in the franchise system, don't buy that franchise. Attempts to change it will likely only backfire.

As an example, here are some tweaks that backfired:

- ☐ A franchisee of a maid service somehow decided that she would not follow the franchisor's advice to use direct mail to advertise her business. Her reason: "Everybody knows direct mail doesn't work." She then concluded that because her profit didn't match those reported by her fellow franchisees,

- the other franchisees must not be telling the truth. She thought she actually would have higher profits since she didn't "waste" money on advertising. The problem was she couldn't build her business without the leads that advertising generates.
- A friend who attended a training session for a recruiting franchise noted one fellow trainee argued every point, insisting he had better ideas for running the franchise. Over time, my friend who followed the system as designed went on to become Rookie of the Year, then Franchisee of the Year. The argumentative know-it-all faded away.
- In another case, one new franchisee decided she wanted to decorate her new massage studio to suit her own tastes rather than use the branded designs of the franchise company. As a result, she missed out on the advantages of branding and spent more on decorating the business. If you think you have a better idea, don't buy that franchise!
- Franchises come with detailed plans for marketing the business. One strategy is to participate in local community events. An academic tutoring franchise we work with suggests that the owner set up a table at local Halloween parades, handing out rulers and key chains for kids, as a way to raise their local profile. When I asked a franchisee who was struggling if she had participated in these events, she admitted she hadn't "gotten around to that yet." No need to say more.

You Can't Fool Yourself

When I first met Evan Birch (a pseudonym), he was a project manager for a financial company with a strong desire to have his own business. When he began the consultation process, we discussed at length the skills he would need for different types of franchise models.

He was soon attracted to an industrial cleaning company that specialized in mold remediation. He liked that people were making good money and that it was relatively easy to build the business because demand for these services is consistent, and competitors tend to be of poor quality. Through his research on this business, he learned the company offered a terrific system and professional services, as well as great support and training. As a result, most franchisees of this business earned a profit in their first year and were taking home six figures by year two. With expectations of matching typical performance, Evan had plenty of money to support the purchase and operating expenses until he could start turning a profit.

I had no doubt Evan could apply his project management skills to the work of this business, but I asked him if he would be able to do the work required to build the business. This entailed getting the name out in the local community and networking with other business owners to generate referrals. Generally speaking, this sort of sales is less confrontational because when you go to local Chamber of Commerce events or industry association meetings, people want to meet you, learn about your business and exchange cards. Evan told me he had done a fair amount of networking in his career, and he was confident he could do what was required to attract referrals and customers.

Evan said he could do it, no sweat, so he bought the franchise. At the time, he had just turned 47 years old and was excited about a new challenge.

After about a year, Evan was struggling and reached out to the franchise company for assistance. As he told me later, he was thrilled with their response. They sent someone out for additional field training with him—at the company's expense. Things went well, and Evan was newly energized about building his business. He said he was committed to doing the networking needed to grow revenue.

Except that, in practice, he continued to avoid the necessary networking. He had the best of intentions and really meant to do the work to introduce people to his services. In the end, however, he was too uncomfortable with a role that required him to generate revenue through his own networking. Just shy of two years in business, he closed his doors.

It turned out Evan had not really been honest with himself. When he started his business, he did not make enough effort to develop contacts. When opportunities arose for networking, he found every excuse not to do the work.

The lesson:

When looking for a business, you have to face the truth about yourself, what you're capable of and what you don't want to do. I'm quite sure Evan was capable of doing the tasks necessary to build his business, but he didn't really want to do them. And so, he didn't. The takeaway: If you don't like parts of the franchise system or don't intend to follow parts of the plan, don't buy the franchise.

We use multiple tools to help people accurately assess their strengths and their abilities, so they can avoid a situation like Evan found himself in. In the end,

*"You may be able to fool others,
but you can't fool yourself."*

SIX

Finding a Quality Franchise

Not all franchises are created equal. Some have far better training and support services, not to mention quality management, that can make the difference between success and failure. The trick is to hitch your wagon to the fastest, strongest horse! That means you have to screen out less-than-ideal businesses to find the right one with the surefire system.

As a prospective franchisee, you need to make good use of all the information that is readily available in order to choose the franchise that is best for you. Most of the information you need is available either in the Franchise Disclosure Document or can be attained through interviews with existing franchise owners. To ensure you make the most educated selection, your top priority before you even consider signing a contract must be a thorough evaluation of the quality and performance of the franchise. Whatever you do, don't let your excitement run away from your reason, which means don't sign any contracts based on superficial knowledge. Your research should go deep and should include advice from the experts.

One important rule of thumb to keep in mind during your due diligence: Everything you hear and learn requires verification.

A good thing about a franchise is that you can test any assumption. You can get all the information you need before you buy a franchise.

You are looking for a franchise that is both high-caliber and well-matched to your specific skills, experience and interests. Over the years, we have developed a method for finding exactly that. Plan on spending a month or two on research, including a review of materials from the franchise companies. As we detail below, your job is to peruse these materials, possibly with the assistance of a good franchise coach, then move on to interviewing existing franchisees, who can show you the way, or possibly warn you off.

Beware of False Assumptions & the Know-It-All

As folks begin to move through their research, I generally suggest they be aware of four hazards that have the potential to short-circuit their research and derail the process. If you keep these in mind, you can avoid getting drawn off course by the psychological traps listed below.

- *Beware of the Know-It-All*
  This is the person in your life who is absolutely certain that the franchise you're looking at is terrible, or may be terrific. They will think they know because they have a tiny bit of information or know someone somewhere who had an experience. But they won't have conducted any real research or have any meaningful data to support their claims.

- *A Case of the Nerves*
  As you go through the process, it's only natural to get nervous about starting a new endeavor. Just remember to trust the process. You'll need to complete a thorough analysis based on the facts you have learned. Then you can make your decision based on facts and logic rather than fear and emotion. Do this and you can complete an effective due diligence that will lead you to a business in which your odds of success are excellent.

- *Becoming Too Skeptical or Not Skeptical Enough*
  When speaking to franchise company representatives, they will inevitably try to sell you on the benefits of their franchise. After all, they're competing for the best of the prospective new franchisees they meet. Don't let this sales pitch put you off. The franchise representatives will provide an abundance of information, and while some may tend to emphasize the rosy over the cautionary, you have the ability to double-check everything they say—which you should do. Listen and learn and, by all means, ask questions. They have valuable information to share with you. In short, listen, then verify.

- *Fear of Change*
  As you get closer to a franchise selection, you might get a creeping feeling of unease. This is common and is caused by fear of change. People generally prefer to stay in their comfort zone, which makes sense unless your present "comfort zone" isn't working for you. We presume this to be true or you wouldn't be looking for a career change. While contemplating and taking steps to change careers can cause a case of the butterflies, you can overcome them by completing your analysis. We recommend you change the way you think about change. Instead of seeing change as a risk, you might notice the advantages of change—change offers you the opportunity to reinvent yourself.

Now you're ready to begin your search for a franchise.

Focus on the Right Issues

When it comes to choosing a business to buy, what matters most is not a competition-free market but, rather, a demonstrated record of success.

Think about it. If there's no competition, it may mean that demand for this type of service or product is insufficient. On the other hand, if you see a number of similar businesses thriving, you could conclude the market is strong for that product or service.

This is why you tend to see a bunch of fast-food restaurants all in a row. We can presume that the real-estate professionals with those companies learned that lots of hungry people pass by this location on a regular basis.

What separates the wheat from the chaff will be the quality of the franchise operating system and business model. The best way to get a good understanding of a new business comes with a franchise. Evaluating an independent business requires a lot of guesswork and finger crossing. Franchises have a complete, established, and transparent process to learn all about the business.

The hard part is making the selection.

Consult a Franchise Coach

You can benefit from the expertise of these professionals who have vetted thousands of franchises, selecting only the best ones, so they can recommend franchises with the greatest chance for success. Even better, this service is free to you. They're paid by the franchise company once a deal is inked. Remember, a franchise coach won't last long unless he's made plenty of matches in which both franchisor and franchisee succeed.

Review Franchise Types

We recommend using a franchise coach before you start perusing the wide array of available franchises. As you will soon see, more than eighty industries representing over 4,000 franchisees comprise the list on the International Franchise Association website at www.franchise.org. They include tutoring centers, all types of B2B services, home services, academic tutoring businesses, personal services and more. You will find opportunities that allow you to work largely on your own, part-time, or build a multi-franchise operation.

After you have narrowed your list to a few select franchises, using the expertise of a franchise coach, you should carefully examine the following features:

Understand the Franchise System

The system is one of the most important components of any franchise. These companies have devoted a great deal of time, energy and expertise into understanding what works and what doesn't in their business. They have developed a system designed for optimum results.

Smart franchise company executives have every incentive to help you. After all, they thrive only if their franchisees succeed. How great is that: a true synergy where they gain only when their franchisees do. The better you succeed, the better they do too!

But the model does no good if the franchisee decides to veer away from the system. While a franchise system is one of the best ways to lower the risk for starting a business, the rule of thumb is you must be willing to follow the system.

The system typically includes:

A Proven Method
As a franchise's key attribute, a good franchise company will continually perfect its system to help their franchisees succeed. They know how many employees you need and what type of advertising works best, how to attract new customers and retain them, and how to manage your costs to help you operate most profitably. The list goes on, depending on the type of business.

Upfront Training
Franchise companies know their training programs are key to your success. This can mean more than fifty hours of supervised instruction, plus more on the job for you and your employees.

Ongoing Support
Most franchise companies have employees whose sole task is to support their franchisees in such areas as IT, sales, advertising, accounting, and human resources. An answer to your question is a mere phone call away. Franchisors may even assign you a particular support point person. In contrast, independent businesses have to hire individual experts for support in each area of their business, and those costs can quickly add up, particularly during the start-up phase.

Don't forget the time you will save. People who start an independent business usually need a couple of months on just the basics before they can open their doors. Simple tasks like creating a logo, a website and the right business card can easily delay your start by two months or more. While that might not seem like a lot, time truly is money. If one of your business goals is to earn yourself a salary of $15,000 a month, a two-month delay in getting started will set you back $30,000.

Guidelines for Setting Up an Office/Store
The franchisor will likely have exact specifications for the type of equipment, fixtures and supplies to purchase, as well as the number of employees you will need. Franchise companies usually develop a specific set of vendors. The time saved not having to do the research on your own for suppliers adds up.

Advertising/Marketing Program
Franchises come with well-developed marketing materials, usually including a website, brochures, and an advertising program. The franchisor will also help you advertise in your own local market, both online and with other recommended services, such as direct mail.

Support on Leasing
If you need a brick-and-mortar location for your business, the franchise company should help you find one that truly works for the business. They know what sort of demographics the area should have, what traffic count helps create success, and when a lease payment is too high.

Once you get a good understanding of the franchise system, you should:

Complete Your Due Diligence

Every potential new franchisee needs to take the time to delve into the details. Whatever you do, read the fine print before signing any contracts.

The good news is that the Federal Trade Commission mandates franchise companies provide their Franchise Disclosure Document (FDD) to prospective franchisees. The FDD is perhaps your most important tool to help you choose the best franchise to match your specialized skills, experience, and preferences. Carefully reading the FDD helps protect you from making a bad choice.

As you pinpoint franchises that you're serious about, you should request a copy of the FDD, which franchisors are required to provide at least fourteen days before you sign a contract or pay any money.

Navigating the FDD takes time, but stick with it. Just remember all the time you put in upfront will reap rewards down the road, especially in helping you avoid costly mistakes. If you don't understand everything you read, find a franchise attorney who can help you.

To help you get started, we've provided a little primer to help you navigate the FDD.

In your review, you should zero in on these key issues:

- **The business history**
  How long has the franchise been in operation?
  Has their core business focus changed in that time?
- **Litigation history**
  A company facing lots of lawsuits may not be a good investment. Be especially wary if you see a number of lawsuits with individual franchise owners.
- **Any earnings claim**
  This is an optional item and very helpful if included.
- **Financial statements**
  Is the franchisor financially healthy?
- **A full accounting of your costs**
  You want to know how much money you'll need.
- **The list of franchisees**

Navigate the 23 Steps to Success

The FDD contains 23 Items, but some are more important than others. One of the most important items for you is **Item 20—the list of outlets**—since, as I already mentioned, the best way to understand any franchise operation is to interview their franchisees, who can provide you an accurate, up-to-the-minute view of what it's like to run this business.

For your first read-through of the FDD, focus on these items:

The Franchisor (Item 1)
The very first page gives you the business history of the franchisor, where it is incorporated, other names under which it has operated, and a general description of the business.

Litigation (Item 3)
You're not looking for a gotcha moment for a single lawsuit, but if you see a history of many lawsuits or arbitration cases brought by franchisees, heed the warning, stop reading, and cross this franchise off your list. Frequent lawsuit activity between the franchisor and franchisees indicates an unusually combative franchisor. If you were foolish enough to join that franchise organization, you should expect them to be just as combative with you, and that's not what you want from the people whose support you are counting on.

Initial Fees and Investment Costs (Items 5-7)
You can learn how much this operation will cost you. How great is that! I can think of no more valuable information than learning exactly how much capital you will need to get your business up and running. By contrast, when you start your own independent business, any number you come up with is, at best, an educated guess.

The cost breakdown will include your initial fees, royalty fees, estimates of wages and other labor costs, training, lease payments, costs to furnish your office or store, inventory, signs, advertising, insurance, etc.

Don't gloss over the numbers. This section will tell you how much money you will need to run your business for several months. Let me repeat. You need enough money to pay your bills until your business becomes profitable and this section will tell you how much that is. Without enough start-up capital, your business could founder.

The one item not included will be how much it will cost you to live until your new business starts turning a profit. Every new business has a ramp-up phase, and you have to be prepared to cover your own living expenses during that period.

Since the number-one reason businesses fail is inaccurately estimating start-up costs, getting the rundown on how much it will cost should enable you to choose a business that actually fits your budget, so you can succeed for the long haul.

Territory (Item 12)
Some franchises have what is called a protected or exclusive territory. This is a promise that they will not allow another franchisee to operate within a specified distance of your location. Franchisors have different ways of determining a territory, which is meant to protect current franchisees but may not be satisfactory to you. Protected

territories are not necessarily better, but you do want to understand the parameters, so you can ensure you have a sufficient market to make a good income.

Earnings Claim *(Item 19)*
Only about a third of all franchises make earnings claims. Since earnings for individual franchises can vary substantially, we recommend you verify any numbers you see in this section with individual franchisees.

List of Franchise Outlets *(Item 20)*
This is where you will find the key that will help you open the door to a successful business future: the names, locations and phone numbers of all franchisees currently operating, as well as franchisees no longer operating. You should call as many as you can, both current and former franchisees, to learn about their businesses. Have the franchisor's support systems been helpful? How long did it take for them to become profitable? Are they satisfied with the franchise? Would they purchase this franchise again? If not, what went wrong?

We recommend you have in-depth conversations with any owners you find who are failing. Sometimes you can learn more from someone who failed than from the biggest success stories. Tips on how best to interview franchisees are covered in the next section.

Financial Statements *(Item 21)*
Franchisors are required to include copies of their audited financial statements for the three most recent fiscal years. Review these to ensure the company is solvent. If you aren't comfortable reading and interpreting the financial statement, then have an accountant look it over to ensure the financial stability of the company. It will be the best $150 you ever spent.

While less important, you should also take note of:

Restrictions *(Items 16-17)*
Franchisors may restrict from whom you order supplies, what you may offer for sale, and where you can sell.

Training *(Item 11)*
While franchisors offer training, you need to know who is eligible for training and who pays. Are new employees eligible? Are support staff available for ongoing support? Again, make sure you know all the costs.

Advertising *(Item 11)*
Franchisees are often asked to contribute a portion of their earnings for advertising. Get the details on what the franchisor requires. Will you need to supplement the national advertising campaign with local advertising? Usually you will, so take that expense into account. Also see Items 6-8.

Before signing any contracts, we recommend you consult a franchise attorney who has the expertise to help you review what can be a long and complex agreement. And do yourself a favor: Make sure the attorney you select specializes in franchising. Only a specialist has the expertise to know exactly what to look for in the franchise contract to protect you.

As you get closer to a decision, you should know:

A Franchisee's Obligations
If you don't agree with all the expectations for how you must operate, this business is not for you. Find this information in Item 9.

Renewal and Termination Procedures
The franchisor is also required to detail how a franchise can be terminated or ownership transferred or renewed. Know these details upfront, because there will come a time when you want to sell, either to retire with your hard-earned wealth, or for a tidy profit. Advice from a franchise attorney is well worth the cost.

Why Franchisees Have Left the System?
With the list of outlets in the FDD (Item 20) you also get contacts for franchisees who have left the system recently. Call them and find out why. If you learn about a pattern of neglect or, perhaps, complaints of wrongful termination of a contract, you might want to back away. Just remember, sometimes the fault lies with the franchisee, and don't take just one person's word for it.

What Current Franchisees Say About the Franchisor?
Your best resource—bar none—are franchisees who can tell you from experience how well the franchisor's services match the hype. Many will even share some of their financial information, such as how long it took to start operating in the black, how much you might realistically be able to earn, etc.

Bottom line: What works for them? Are they making money? Are they happy with the program?

While your research may take some time, and expert advice may add some expense, the payoff is in the end result:

> *You can choose a great franchise. One*
> *that gives you the life and the living you always wished for,*
> *and that works for you in the long run.*

Interviewing Your Way to Success

Once you have read through the FDD, where you can get the list of franchisees, you should start calling them. You can learn from no better source how the franchisor's system works. Besides all the issues mentioned above, we have a list of questions in the appendix, which you should consult and use as a worksheet when calling franchisees. Keeping a good record of your interviews will allow you to compare and contrast what you hear from different people, considering their locations and specific aspects of their personal experience.

As we mentioned, you should also make a point to talk to franchisees who have not been successful. Find out what went wrong. Remember, sometimes people shortchange their research process and choose franchises that don't suit their expertise, interests, or personality, and this can cause failure as much as problems stemming from the franchisor.

Every good interview follows the same basic steps. Ask a friend to help you practice before you begin to locate, contact and interview your way to the right franchise.

A Critical Opportunity to Verify the FDD
The FDD includes many financial estimates, and interviewing franchisees is your opportunity to verify them. You can ask the owners what their average revenues are for franchise units after one, two, or three years and what their profit margins are. You can also confirm the amount of investment the franchise requires. Pay particularly close attention to how accurate the franchisor's claims are in the FDD.

Don't be surprised if many franchise owners cannot answer questions about costs or profit margins. Not everyone who becomes an owner knows those figures, but you should be able to find some owners who are very familiar with their financial metrics and are willing to share their observations with you.

If you have trouble locating franchisees with this type of knowledge, ask the franchisor to direct you to someone who is able to help answer these crucial questions. And if you don't know exactly what to ask to get the information you are seeking, ask your franchise coach for a tip.

Be Cordial and Gracious
Remember you are imposing on the franchisee's time, so when you call, get right to the point: You are interested in the franchise and are hoping he or she might have a few minutes to talk about his or her experiences. Ask if this is a good time or when might be a good time to call back. Often, it will work well to email the franchisees in order to schedule a specific time to talk together.

Plan Your Interview
You might want to plan a couple of layers to your interview. First, prepare a few questions that would take no more than fifteen minutes of the franchisee's time. Then write additional questions you might get to if the franchisee does have the time. Ask questions that you want answered specifically by a franchisee—what this person knows that you cannot otherwise learn from any prepared written material. In other words, don't waste their time on questions easily answered by the franchisor's promotional materials.

Show Respect

You may not like everything the franchisees tell you, but you're after their perspective. For owners who may be struggling, the most important information you want to get is whether they are following the franchisor's system. How do you learn this? By the time you are having this conversation, you will know the components of the franchise system.

If owners of a particular franchise are directed to spend $2,000 per month on advertising, you will want to ask each owner how much they spend. If they tell you, "Everybody knows advertising doesn't work, so I don't advertise," you have found the reason they aren't successful.

Listen

The most important time during your interview is when you're not talking. Try to draw out as much information as possible from the franchisee by asking succinct questions, and then stop talking. Sometimes people need a few moments to clarify their thoughts before responding.

Clarify

Even with the best listening skills, you may miss some of what is said. Don't be shy about asking your source to repeat something or clarify an answer you may not have understood. As most journalism professors will tell you, there's no such thing as a stupid question. Worse is skipping the question you wish you had asked.

Make sure you ask for specific examples, evidence, which can help you understand the story better. For example, when you ask, "Did a franchisor's actions live up to their promises?" make sure you learn how and in what circumstances they did or didn't. But be careful not to turn your friendly conversation into an interrogation.

Follow-Up

As you go through your notes and something important pops out that you fear you may have misunderstood or gotten wrong in your notes, call back. Most people appreciate conscientious attempts to get it right. Just remember to be respectful of the franchisee's time. And it never hurts to drop a thank-you email after the interview. You might want to keep these lines of communication open for the future.

Specific Questions for Franchisees

1. ***Why did you choose this franchise?***
   Listen for: Does the franchisee have anything in common with you? Can you see yourself in his or her shoes? Do you have the skills necessary to run this business?

2. ***Have you been satisfied with the level of support and training from the franchisor?***
   Was it all that the franchisor promised? Do the support staff and executives of the franchisor know their stuff? Are they easy to work with?

3. *What do you like best and least about the business?*
   Get a good feel for what running this business is all about. Maybe the best thing is the social interaction with customers. If you don't want to deal with the public, that sort of need for connection could indicate this franchise won't suit you. Choosing a business can be a lot like choosing a spouse. The match has to be particular to you.

4. *Would you purchase this franchise again?*
   If the answer is no, find out why. These reasons may not be true for you.

5. *How long should it take to reach break-even?*
   You need to know how much capital it would take to get this business to profitability.

6. *Are you able to earn six figures with this business?*
   While you may not be able to get specifics on their earnings, press for as much information as you can to see how it aligns with the franchisor's sales pitch. Getting information on earnings from franchisees is a critical aspect of your research. Why? They're the only source from which you can get actual numbers because franchisor executives are prohibited from discussing detailed financial information with you.

7. *What are the keys to success?*
   In most businesses, to become successful, some features of operating the business matter more than others. For example, business success might hinge more directly on developing employees, networking in your local community or managing the advertising programs. Make sure you understand which aspects of the business matter most in the franchise you are considering.

8. *What do you spend most of your day doing?*
   Learning what the owners focus their time on can help you understand if this is the right business match for you. Maybe the workdays of successful owners are largely spent on sales activities, such as networking. If that is not your skill or interest, then this franchise might not be the right one for you. As we often point out, the role of the owner should closely match your skills and interests.

Determine if a Franchise Operation Matches the Hype

The stories are legion about people who have breathed new life into their careers with a franchise or even several franchises. But there are also some pretty notable misses in the franchise business, as well. Just think Quiznos or Curves, two franchise systems which have faltered for different reasons: Quiznos, the once promising sandwich shop, fell into bankruptcy and Curves, fitness centers for women of a certain size, is a shadow of its former self.

While it's true that nothing in life is guaranteed, you can do quite a bit to minimize your risk by thoroughly checking into a franchisor's track record. As we discussed previously, you must always include in your research a thorough reading of the FDD. Or, if you know you're not likely to read it, ask someone else to read it for you. Better still, have the FDD reviewed by an attorney who specializes in franchising.

Item 20 of the FDD tells you both how many people have joined the franchise as new owners and how many have left. If you see a franchise that is not growing, or more alarming, getting smaller, you will want to understand why.

STORY FROM THE FIELD

How In-Depth Due Diligence Led to Success

Rachel Tilow took her time while searching for her second franchise business, determined to spend as much time on research as it took to feel comfortable with her decision to commit to a new business. She knew from experience how good it feels to be in a business you love. Likewise, she had seen her share of struggling franchisees and knew problems often stem from leaping before looking.

Tilow enjoyed the sixteen years she spent as a successful franchisee of Gymboree, a parent-child play center, that she had often visited when her son was a toddler. When she moved to Tampa, Fla., she went looking for a Gymboree and couldn't find one. So she opened one of her own.

But not before conducting a thorough vetting of the company.

Even though she loved the whole concept, she did her due diligence, taking a full year from when she started investigating the franchise business to her opening day. During her research, she talked to many of the already existing franchisees. She knew she wanted to make money and have a flexible schedule, so she could spend time with her young son.

When she bought in, she was franchise No. 184, and when she sold the franchise sixteen years later in 2005, there were more than 500 franchisees. Gymboree has evolved to include a large retail business, but back when she first bought, Gymboree was a play center that offered mom and baby classes.

As a franchisee, Tilow loved having the ability to share ideas with her network of fellow franchisees. After she sold, Tilow continued in business, first as a landlord and property manager, then the owner of a produce business. After relocating to another city, she decided to look into buying another franchise business.

This time she reviewed a couple of franchise companies to start. The first franchise on her list didn't seem exactly forthcoming when answering her questions.

"They were awful at communicating with me," Tilow said, and when she asked for the Franchise Disclosure Document, "I had to request it six times before they actually sent it."

The upshot: "I didn't trust the franchisor." So, she moved on to investigate the next one.

This was a tax preparation business that promised franchisees would need only to work three months of the year to make enough for the entire rest of the year. After talking to twenty franchisees—incidentally, way more than most people call—she learned the sales pitch didn't hold up to scrutiny.

When her franchise coach mentioned The Groutsmith, of Sarasota, Florida, Tilow immediately had an interest in the basic, no-frills business of grout cleaning and restoration.

Since her top goal was to make money, she called every franchise, other than those related to the owners, which was just under thirty-five in this small operation, and she learned "they were all making money right off the bat. They raved about the franchise. No one had anything negative to say.

Content with what she had learned, Tilow bought in and became franchise owner No. 36. This time, her entire investigation process, from start to decision, took her only five weeks.

The Groutsmith system allows franchisees to keep their overhead low, Tilow noted, and she keeps her office in her home and rents a small storage unit. She has one employee, who started part-time then moved to full-time as soon as the business grew enough to fill the hours, about ten weeks after they opened. Just as the other franchisees told her, Tilow started making money pretty quickly and started paying herself a salary when she was only two weeks in.

She says the franchise company always has someone available when she calls with a question. "They are extremely supportive," she said, plus her fellow franchisees are also a great source of support.

The key to doing well with a franchise business is to understand exactly what you're getting into, so that when you start your business you already know this is a business model you can follow. Then you need to follow it.

> *"People buy franchises and they just think*
> *they have a better idea of how to run the business,"*
> *she observed, then added,*
> *"but that's a recipe for failure."*

As part of your preparation, you will talk to representatives from the franchise company. Most franchisors have a standard protocol for potential new franchisees that includes in-person and telephone meetings with selected executives, as well as lots of reading materials to introduce you to the franchisor's system. For many franchise companies, the process culminates in Franchise Discovery Day, where you visit a franchisor at its headquarters, meet the support staff, and make your final decision on whether this franchise is for you.

You should use this opportunity to zero in on the issues that are critical to helping a new franchisee succeed. Get a feel for the corporate climate and how attentive they are to franchisees' needs.

The nitty-gritty financial issues are best left to your interviews with franchisees, who are allowed to answer any question you pose. Regulations prohibit executives of franchisors from giving you any financial information other than what is already in the FDD. You can get more details, but the franchisees will be the ones to provide them. They can tell you how quickly revenues build, what level of revenue most people reach, and how profitable the franchise is.

During this process, you will have ample opportunity to reassess and decide whether this franchise is or isn't for you, either because you don't connect to the business or its executives, or you've decided the business isn't a match for your skills and background.

STORY FROM THE FIELD

Selecting a Franchise is a Mutual Vetting Process
ARCpoint Comes with a Whole Team Rooting for You!

What do you think is the number-one goal of the most successful franchise companies? If you answer recruiting franchisees, you would be wrong. Like any other company, franchisors want to make as much money as possible. The difference is a franchise company needs good franchisees to accomplish this goal. They want to recruit only those franchisees who can help them make money. As a result, they're scouting for franchisees that provide the best match for their business.

This is why buying into an effective franchise system can be such a win-win proposition.

The new franchisee gets to recharge his or her career, while the franchise company works to attract highly qualified, talented professionals to its ranks. The simple fact is the better franchisees perform, which is often connected to how good their support and training is, the more money everyone makes.

How well franchisees learn and execute the franchisor's time-tested system is critical to their success. As a result, franchisors place a high priority on the franchise selection process because the better the match, the more successful both parties will be.

"We're very selective when we grant a license to franchises," said Randy Loeb, vice president of franchise development for ARCpoint Labs, a Greenville, South Carolina-based company, which offers wellness programming and drug, alcohol, DNA, and forensic testing.

Besides relying on franchise consultants or coaches to bring them well-qualified candidates, ARCpoint uses a written test to vet prospective franchisees for the right "entrepreneurial skill sets," Loeb said.

According to Loeb, when a franchise inquiry comes in, "We give each candidate an electronic brochure and walk them through the business model." After they sufficiently understand ARCpoint's business, within about seven to ten days, they will complete the assessment, which consists of multiple-choice questions that take ten to fifteen minutes to complete. ARCpoint uses the assessment to evaluate entrepreneurial skills, such as leadership, time management, and "consultative" sales ability, which is about learning from clients what their businesses needs are and working to fulfill them.

"We teach our franchisees how to go in and save them money," Loeb said. "If the prospective franchisee doesn't meet ARCpoint's qualifications, I suggest they look at another franchise that may be a better fit for them," Loeb said.

"ARCpoint is probably one of the most sophisticated business models in franchising today," he said. Consequently, they want people who can excel with their business model.

"We're looking for quality folks, who will effectively represent the brand," he added. Primarily a sales and marketing business, the company's emphasis is on finding somebody who has sales and marketing experience.

After the franchise candidate makes the decision to join ARCpoint, Loeb said, it's all about the training.

"We spoon-feed them," Loeb said, referring to their method, which allows franchisees to master one component of the system before moving onto the next training module. They implement each module, one at a time, and when they've learned it thoroughly, they move on to the next.

In addition, the company hosts several monthly webinars to give franchisees updates, improve their skills, and stay current with testing rules and regulations.

"We have a very detailed rollout," he said. "We automatically know early if something is wrong so appropriate changes can be made to help franchisees succeed."

This whole approach keeps the franchisee on track, following the system, which is a critical component to their success.

"We're bird dogging franchise owners all the time to make sure they're following the system," Loeb said.

"Franchisees succeed because our system works."

At the time of our conversation, ARCpoint had more than one hundred franchises open and one hundred more territories sold and scheduled to open. Over time, most franchisees end up with multiple territories. The company doesn't actively encourage franchisees to buy additional territories, but many like the economies of scale, Loeb explained.

The franchise operation is a two-way street. Both parties have to get something out of the arrangement. This is why the match is so important.

"There are a lot of smart people with doctorates who've taken the assessment and failed. Just because you're smart doesn't mean this will be the right fit for you," Loeb said. "Sometimes I get folks who fall in love with what we do, and then I pull the rug out from under them because it's not a good fit."

"It's not personal," he explained. The company only wants to avoid franchisees who struggle

> *"We're interested in the quality of the owner, not putting another notch on our belt."*

For prospective franchisees, I cannot emphasize enough how important it is that the franchise follow some sort of vetting process. Yes, there are franchisors whose only method for screening new franchisees is to check if they have a pulse, but they don't do their new franchisees any favors. Or themselves.

The best franchise companies will make a point to help prospective franchisees understand what it takes to succeed with their business to help ensure it's a good match for both parties. This process saves a lot of heartache down the road for both franchisee and franchisor.

Another franchise company that uses a profiler program is Money Mailer, a direct mail marketing franchise company. When we spoke about this, they were using a 90-minute online program that cost the company $200 per profile.

For Money Mailer, if the prospective franchisee doesn't do well on the test, it's not necessarily disqualifying. Some issues require extra training, said Dennis Jenkins, vice president of franchise licensing. "We probably reject about one-third of people interested in Money Mailer. If they're 80 percent certain about the franchise, we bring them to a Discovery Day, and of those that come, 80 percent sign an agreement to become franchisees."

Preparing for a Franchise Discovery Day

Before going to a Discovery Day, you may have spent a month or two on your due diligence, possibly with the assistance of a franchise coach. Once you've narrowed down your search to maybe one or two franchises, you've probably talked to their executives multiple times, likely read introductory materials and/or completed online tutorials.

During this time, you've gotten to know the ins and outs of the business and how exactly the franchise system works. By the time you make the decision to attend a Discovery Day, you're pretty close to making a purchase. Or you wouldn't be there.

At a Discovery Day, both parties strive to get an impression of each other. The franchise company will see if you bring a serious professional intention and knowledge of the business. And you'll be checking out their operations, their executives, their support services, and whether you feel you could work closely with their team.

STORY FROM THE FIELD

Discovery Day Clinches It

When Megan Yu, of Ann Arbor, Michigan, graduated from Michigan State University with a bachelor's degree in retailing, she knew she wanted to own her own business one day. To start out, she went to work as a manager of a retail store.

The opportunity to actually become her own boss arose when her father, Andy Yu, an engineer, decided to retire and offered to partner with her in a business.

Megan, then 28, and her father, 56, began methodically setting goals and parameters for their search.

Andy said their first step was meeting with a business broker in their area. After not finding an existing independent business suitable to their needs, they switched their search to the franchise sector and spent six months researching different franchises.

"For us, it was a focus on longevity and stability," Megan said, adding that lifestyle was also a key consideration. They knew they were looking for a business that would operate Monday through Friday, with an occasional Saturday by appointment.

"My Dad, being an engineer, likes having a product, seeing the fruits of his labor," she said.

As they started weighing some of the elements involved in running a business, they appreciated the benefits of buying a franchise, most notably that it has an established track record and comes with its own operating system.

"The way we looked at it is we want to run a business," said Andy. "We don't want to get into all these miscellaneous details that will consume all our time and effort. We can focus on our value-added work."

Rather than research the best machinery, equipment and office furnishings, and negotiate the best lease agreement, areas where they lacked experience, they could rely on the franchise company's expertise and networks. As a result, they were free to focus their time on activities, likes sales and marketing, that have more direct impact on the bottom line.

Before long, Megan and Andy had narrowed their search to two different sign companies. Finally, the choice came down to an intangible factor: Which franchise support team did they have a better connection with?

That meant attending Franchise Discovery Day at company headquarters, where franchise company executives and prospective franchisees get a chance to get to know each other up close and personal and decide if going into business together is a good idea. Attending a Discovery Day is generally the last step before deciding whether to purchase a franchise or not.

During a Discovery Day at company headquarters, Megan was greeted by her "host" at her hotel and taken to company headquarters, where she met with current franchisees, as well as corporate's support staff. Next, she toured a brand-new training facility, all of which convinced Megan that this was the business for her.

"It's beneficial to meet the people we've been talking to on the phone, so you can establish a personal connection," Andy said.

> *"It was the people I met through the course of the program,"* Megan added. *The one-on-one interactions with the owners. That was huge."*

Franchise Discovery Day will either captivate you with a display of stellar services and support staff, or you'll discover something about the franchisor that sends you to the exit with a queasy feeling of doubt. For example, you may find the CEO has recently changed and you're not sure about the transition. Or perhaps, you'll discover you don't like the support staff. You want to learn as much as you can about the franchise company before Discovery Day, so you can spend the day getting to know the people you will be working with. As Andy noted of Discovery Day, "I wouldn't say we learned anything new."

That's because they had done their homework.
Before you even arrive for Franchise Discovery Day, you should have:

Performed a Comparison study
Look at a few business types that might suit your experience, interests, and lifestyle.

Read the Franchise Disclosure Document
Federal law requires franchise companies to disclose much useful data, from a list of all their franchises to detailed financial information. Read through this carefully.

Researched the Market
You should be confident this business type will work in your location.

Talked to the Franchisees
Interview as many as possible to hear about the franchise company's support systems and whether they've worked for them.

When you arrive at Franchise Discovery Day, you should be armed with highly educated questions that will enable you to learn if this really is the team you want behind your new business.

Here's a window into what you as a potential new franchisee should expect before a Discovery Day:

The Franchisor's Courtship

Financial Pre-requisites
Franchisors will assess whether you qualify to become a franchisee in their program. This starts with determining if you meet the minimum net worth and liquidity requirements. Expect the franchise company to go further. The best will want to be certain you understand the franchise model and that you have the skills and desire to follow their model.

Forms to Complete
These may include a personality profile or a questionnaire.

A series of Seminars
Franchisors will typically set up a series of phone calls or webinars, in which you'll speak to experts inside the company to educate you about their business. You should expect about one to two hours a week for the calls and lots more time for homework, which may include reading materials, such as the Franchise Disclosure Document and an assignment to speak to franchisees. As the potential investor, you set the pace. The process can take from one to three months, and you'll have ample opportunity to get to know their team.

Invitation to a Discovery Day
By this time, you understand the nature of the business and exactly what owners do every day. The franchisor should have decided whether you have what it takes to be successful as one of their franchisees. If you've been invited to a Discovery Day, odds are you're as interested in the franchise company as they are in you—and you're almost ready to make your decision. You may already have consulted a franchise attorney.

Discovery Day
You will travel to corporate headquarters and may join a small group of other prospective franchisees for a day full of meetings, including time with key executives, where you will have a chance to get to know each other up close and personal.

While a franchise company still has the prerogative to reject you, once you've made it to Discovery Day, the odds are in your favor.

At the end of the day, you should have learned:

- Whether adequate support infrastructure is actually in place
- What the training program consists of
- Whether the executives interested in you?
- Whether you establish a good rapport with them

Only by participating in this thorough process can you be sure you're ready to take on such an important commitment. Usually at the end of this process, you've either decided you want to become one of their franchisees or that this franchise isn't for you.

STORY FROM THE FIELD

A Franchise Discovery Day, A Franchisor's Perspective

"A Chance to Make the Intangible Tangible"

While prospective franchisees are most interested in discovering whether this business model can work for them, when Discovery Day arrives, the franchisor is also assessing whether the prospective franchisee is up to snuff. As we have emphasized, a franchise in many ways is like a partnership, where the franchise company offers a business model, expertise, training and ongoing support and the franchisee provides matching skills and experience, ingenuity, diligence and perseverance to get a new business up and running.

Both of you have a vested interest in the franchise succeeding: You want to make a good living, and the franchise company wants to protect its brand name and maximize its own profitability.

As one executive of a large franchisor of several different franchise brands said, "Discovery Day allows the executives with the franchisor a chance to meet and spend a little time with the franchisees to see if it's a good fit."

By the time Franchise Discovery Day arrives, one of their executives will have already had meetings with the prospective franchisee, preferably in person, and taken that person through a process to learn about the business model.

"Discovery Day allows the franchisee to gain a complete picture of the support network and the value that is typically unseen by a typical franchisee in the field."

People generally discover whether the business is a good fit as they go through the process, he said. "If you can't follow these steps, you aren't likely to follow the franchise system itself," he added.

> *"To be successful, it's not about reinventing the wheel,*
> *but rather following the model," he noted.*

This franchise company sees hundreds of people a year at a Discovery Day, and everyone who comes through gets individual attention. By the time they arrive, they tend to be very interested.

As a result of this process, the vast majority of their franchisees are successful.

While their franchisees come from a variety of backgrounds, they all tend to share an entrepreneurial spirit.

"The best franchisees come from a corporate background, so they understand structure, but they have an entrepreneurial spirit and they want to control their own destiny," he said, referring to his own particular franchise brands.

No matter their background, all their franchisees understand that the benefits of a franchise enable them to get their new business off the ground quickly, thanks to a good launch process, training, and support.

"With an independent business, you have to find all your own equipment, vendors, location, hire employees, learn how it all works, figure out your pricing, and that's before you even sell a thing—a lot of expense and time," he said. "We can take you through that a lot faster, and that gives you a head-start."

> *While you have your checklist,*
> *it's good to remember so does a franchisor—*
> *reassurance that the company is working to create the*
> *best possible conditions for success.*

Nine Key Questions to Ask Franchisors

How Much is the Full Investment in the Franchise?
These numbers will be broken down and listed in the FDD, but you want to hear what the franchisor has to say on the subject. If they try to sugarcoat the costs in any way that doesn't match your background research, keep digging until you are confident you know what the actual costs should be.

Franchise owners are a great source for this information. You always want to be sure you understand the real-world truths. After all, one of the worst positions you can find yourself in is to have run out of capital before your business becomes profitable.

What is the Background of Company Executives?

While this information will be listed in Items 1-3 of the FDD, the executives who oversee support and training will probably not be covered in these materials. Ask them about themselves, their background, their approach to training, the best ways franchisees learn to succeed. Remember, these are the people you will be interacting with on a regular basis, especially at the beginning. Get a sense of who these people are, then follow your gut. If you feel someone isn't being genuine or truthful with you, stay away.

How Old and Established is the Franchise?

Ask executives about how the company has evolved and, ideally, improved over the years. If it's a fairly new franchise, what are the company's plans for growth?

What is the Success Rate of Franchisees?

They may give you a rosy window into franchisee success, but if you prepared by reading about any claims the company may have made in the FDD, you can ask good questions. You should also be more knowledgeable if you've already interviewed franchisees for whom you can find contact information in the FDD.

What Type of Training Program Does the Franchisor Offer?

How much ongoing support will you get? Are particular executives assigned to your region? Will you always be able to get someone on the phone for a consultation? As you learn where the greatest opportunities and challenges are for any franchise, you should find out about the level of support in those areas.

What Exactly is Involved with the System?

A thorough understanding of the system takes time and research. You will want to determine if this is a system you can follow. Is the system sufficient to help you achieve success? Sometimes, newer franchises may still be working out the kinks.

Before you decide on a particular franchise, you should understand how you would operate it if you were one of the franchisees. Getting a real handle on all this information is the central focus of your process of discovery.

If Things Go Badly for a New Franchisee, What Does the Franchisor Do to Help?

Is there a triage system of some kind? Good franchisors should have adequate support to help if and when you hit a few stumbling blocks.

How are Territories Determined?

As mentioned earlier, if territories are too close together or too small, you may not be able to capture enough sales to be successful. Be sure you have asked franchisees if the territory rules give them a large enough market to achieve the revenues they desire.

What's Involved in Selling a Franchise?

Sometime down the road you will likely want to sell your franchise, either because you want to retire or you're ready to pocket a tidy profit from your thriving business.

Selling a franchise is generally similar to selling any private business—with a few differences.

While you should understand the procedure with the specific franchise you're interested in, the process generally works like this:

The Owner Needs to Find a Buyer.
The franchisee can sign on with a business broker or advertise himself. What can be helpful is that many franchisors will promote the business as a resale to anyone inquiring about franchise availability in that particular region. With some franchises, other franchisees looking to expand might be your most likely buyers.

The Prospective Buyer Researches the Opportunity.
Similar to your own due diligence, this likely will include a review of the financials of your existing business.

The Buyer and Seller Negotiate a Price and the Terms.
If they reach an agreement, they will both sign a letter of intent.

The Buyer Looks for Financing.
There are lenders eager to provide financing for franchise resales. Since the business is already profitable, the lender will usually consider this a low-risk loan.

The Franchisor Needs to Approve the Buyer.
As a franchisee, you are well aware of the importance of this step since any good franchisor wants owners who understand and will follow the franchise system. The potential new owner will be vetted by the franchisor. Do they have the right skills? Are they adequately capitalized? Will they follow the system?

The New Owner Will Need to Sign the Franchise Agreement.
Sometimes they will sign the exact same agreement as the selling owner did or they will sign the current version, which may be different. The buyer has the opportunity to have a lawyer review the agreement.

The Buyer Pays the Seller
And they both sign off on an asset purchase agreement.

The Transaction is Complete.
The buyer now owns the business, and the seller has the money.

SEVEN

Solid Trends in Franchising
Stay away from the next new craze!

Choosing a franchise has to be a far more substantive process than jumping on the next big wave. For example, cupcakes were all the rage in 2016, and while they make a pretty window, their long-term appeal was fleeting. Frozen yogurt also made a strong comeback after almost disappearing some years ago. But it doesn't take much to saturate the market, and you know it's a fad when it fizzles out fast.

What's hot and what's not may be a typical topic at the annual auto show, but you want to stay away from fads when it comes to franchises. Sort of like the flavor of the month, when folks get tired of it, they stop buying. After all, people are not likely to buy specialty cupcakes on a regular basis or continue buying frozen yogurt when the weather turns cold, which is why these businesses tend to come and go as often as the weather changes.

Everyone always seems to be looking for the next big thing, but the smart money is on the long-term trend—in franchising as much as any other business. Rather than cruise your neighborhood to ascertain the types of businesses most in demand, look to the larger economic trends to guide your search for a new business.

A strong business idea fulfills a deep-seated market need, which, as we know, some people may have not yet realized. Who would ever have guessed 20 years ago that Americans would now be so addicted to their espresso drinks!

Choosing a business in which to invest your hard-earned savings and labor requires as much of your business acumen as you will apply to operating your future business.

We like businesses with either of these two sets of characteristics: businesses that succeed even in economic downturns or those that capitalize on our new economy. The International Franchise Association data has consistently shown commercial and residential services to be strong growth areas.

Look for the Tried and True

Some of the best opportunities are with franchises in well-established markets, where the field may already seem crowded. But there's a lot to be said for the tried and true. After all, savvy buyers choose the economic sectors with consistent growth.

Look for businesses that tend to be recession resistant, not easily outsourced overseas or not vulnerable to internet competition. Examples include firms that conduct workplace drug and alcohol testing, mandated by the government for some industries, and companies specializing in the restoration of water-damaged homes.

Services Always in Demand

Senior Care
As we all know, the baby boomers are swelling the ranks of senior citizens, setting a great growth trajectory for senior care. Several excellent franchisors operate and thrive in this segment. See the next section for more details.

Health Care
The healthcare industry has experienced excellent growth in recent years. As baby boomers age, the prospects for the future may be even better. You can find franchises that provide home health care, operate wellness clinics, or offer wellness services to a business's employees to help keep employees at work, rather than the doctor's office.

Hair Salons
People are always going to need haircuts, and several good franchises exist in this niche.

Pet Services and Supplies
The trend of people treating their pets with the same loving care as they treat their children probably isn't going away anytime soon. This phenomenon of people doting on their pets extends to all sorts of high-end goods and services.

Home Repair
In a modern variation of the old saying, your home is your castle, statistics show spending continues strong for products and services to keep those homes up to date for modern living. Gains in remodeling activity are expected to continue to be strong in the next several years, according to the Leading Indicator of Remodeling Activity. So long as people need a place to live, home repair and maintenance businesses should continue growing.

Companies that retrofit homes for accessibility
Far more older people are staying in their homes well into their very old age, and those homes often require retrofits such as wheelchair ramps or stair lifts.

Property Damage Repair
No matter the rate of unemployment or growth in GDP, natural disasters will continue to occur, and families whose homes have been damaged by fire, flood and hurricane will require cleanup.

Services That Capitalize on Economic Trends

Temporary Staffing
In this age of downsizing and increasing automation, many companies now routinely use contract workers and temp staffing project-by-project.

IT Support
As an integral aspect of 21st-century business, most small businesses outsource their IT support, and some excellent franchises have risen to fulfill this need.

Business Coaching
Business owners are always looking for an edge and for ways to improve their operations. Increasingly, they turn to business coaches for guidance on how to solve business problems and take advantage of opportunities.

Why do these professions remain strong even in weak economies? Uncertain times cause more business owners and executives to look for help and advice.

Digital Advertising
As the "Mad Men" age of advertising fades into distant memory and social media is now king, lots of established businesses need help in reorienting their advertising strategy toward the digital sphere.

Feel-Good Franchising

Giving back to society while making a living often becomes a goal for mid-career changers who want to shift their lives to focus on ways to contribute to the greater good. While they may be looking for solid six figure incomes, they want to feel that the work they do benefits others.

When rethinking their careers, they're often interested in finding balance in their lives.

If you're the type of person who has always wanted a career that allowed you to do well and do good, lots of franchises exist for you. Examples include tutoring, health and wellness, or helping people cope with aging. You can find a franchise to help you advance your career while satisfying your spiritual or altruistic goals.

We see these sort of businesses particularly interest people who enjoy managing others. If you like to mentor and develop your staff, a coaching business might have a lot of appeal to you. Are you strong in getting your team to work together to achieve a goal? Many business owners and managers are very willing to pay for the type of insight you can bring. And a franchise can show you how to market your services to them.

If you hate spending your days looking at spreadsheets full of numbers or selling the latest throwaway widgets from China and wish you could have a direct impact on people's lives, remember, a franchise can give you the tools you need to succeed in this entirely new line of work.

Capitalize on the Growth in the Senior Care Business

While a distinct economic trend, senior care can also satisfy your desire to do good in the marketplace. In this burgeoning business, the expertise provided by franchise companies can make all the difference to success.

You don't need any particular knowledge about geriatrics to get into senior care, and with a franchise, you get all the training and ongoing support to teach you what you need to succeed.

As baby boomers get older, increasingly they want to age in place, and eventually many will need in-home care to help them do so, which is why the business of senior care has done so well in recent years. Home health care and personal care aides are among the country's fastest growing occupations, expected to grow by 38 percent in ten years, according to the Bureau of Labor Statistics.

As a result, senior care can be the perfect place for budding entrepreneurs to find a new career niche.

STORY FROM THE FIELD

If You Prefer Management, There's a Franchise for That, Too!

Many franchise companies offer franchises in regional management, in which the franchisee performs many of the franchisor's tasks for a specific geographic region. In this position, you help create a productive network of franchisees in that region. You will recruit, and train new franchisees then tutor them as they work to get their businesses up and running. This is usually called a Master Franchise or an Area Representative Franchise.

Always Best Care (ABC) is a great example of this model. In the interest of full disclosure, my partner, Ken Garron, and I were area representatives for ABC in the Philadelphia area, until selling our franchise back to the franchisor.

The area representative recruits new franchisees
then works to help them succeed.
There is an incentive built into the relationship
since the better the franchisees perform,
the more money the area representative earns.

For ABC, the most significant challenges new owners face is finding customers and staffing cases, so they can provide care for their clients. Our first goal as area representatives was always to ensure prospective franchisees fully understand their role before they would buy the franchise.

We would make sure the prospective owner was a good fit for the business. This helped us recruit only franchisees who would be successful. It also reassured our prospective franchisees, since they knew that if we invited them to come on board, we must have confidence in their ability to succeed.

After the new franchise owner signs on, the area rep helps them prepare to open. For example, first the franchisees must identify where in their community people get care. Generally, they'll be looking for skilled nursing facilities, primarily those that specialize in short-term care. People in these facilities will usually be going home soon and may need care when they get there.

Prospective franchisees are brought through a very specific process that includes:

Research - in which you learn about the business model

In the case of ABC, for example, the franchisor advises new franchisees what their first weeks will look like. They will call on the skilled nursing facilities every week, meet with the social worker, and develop a relationship with these people so that they can earn referrals. Prospective franchisees are told they may have to visit the nursing facilities for a couple of months before a social worker will start making referrals to them. During that time, they will have proved themselves credible, that they can work hard and are worthy of taking care of their patients.

At this stage, the area representative acts as a kind of reality check, to help prevent a poor match with a prospective franchisee. When prospective owners learn all that is involved, they may decide the business is not the right one for them. We consider that a successful research process.

If they are not a good fit for the business, it is much better that they learn this before they make an investment.

Pre-Training Preparation

Once the contract is signed, the first step is working through ABC's pre-training checklist, which has 85 items. New franchisees complete the items on the checklist before attending their week-long classroom training. During this period, the franchise company helps new franchisees get their insurance and state-required license.

Each state has different requirements, and the franchise company's experts can save new franchisees a lot of time avoiding mistakes in the application process. The franchise offers the additional advantage of connecting new franchisees with an insurance company that will write them a liability policy. Most insurance companies won't provide liability coverage for a new health care business. But they do for a new franchisee who is joining a well-established business.

The advertising department will set up your website, and you will order brochures and business cards from existing templates. You will also set up your office to meet HIPAA requirements (Health Insurance Portability and Accountability Act).

The franchisee's area rep calls every day during the three weeks of pre-training to help answer any questions and guide the new franchisee through the process.

Classroom Training at the Company Headquarters
New franchisees go to headquarters for one business week, where they receive classroom training, as well as time in the field. They spend a day visiting existing referral accounts to see what this process feels like. They will also spend time with senior executives and local support staff.

Training in the Field
The field training in their home territories is a minimum of three days. New franchisees spend time with their area rep, knocking on doors together at hospitals, rehabilitation facilities and doctor's offices.

"Let them know there's a new guy in town," Garron said, adding "I'd go out with them as much as they wanted," noting that typically means a couple of days more than the franchise request before the owners are on their own. After the field training, I would often speak to new franchisees several times per week. They call, or I check in. Since everybody's income is connected, everyone works together to maximize success.

Franchisees in our region also got an opportunity to share their stories and get support from fellow franchisees at regional meetings three times a year. The point is they should always feel there's a team behind them.

When you start your own business,
you're not in it by yourself.

EIGHT

The Veteran Advantage
*Franchisors offer incentives to help
military veterans who start their own franchises*

If you're a military veteran, the International Franchise Association (IFA) thinks you're particularly well-equipped for a franchise, and they established a program to help you take the leap into entrepreneurship and a career in which you can use the skills and discipline you acquired in the military.

VetFran was founded as a special program within the IFA in 1991 to help veterans returning from the first Gulf War as a way to thank veterans for their service. Veterans from any era can learn how to apply the skills they acquired in the military to the business of a franchise.

To advance the program further, in 2011, the IFA launched Operation Enduring Opportunity, a partnership with several organizations, including the US Chamber of Commerce and the US Department of Veterans Affairs, to help the large influx of veterans transitioning to civilian life get into franchise careers. The program has been a great success.

Through VetFran, many franchisors will waive 10 to 25 percent of the franchise fee, which can help veterans hire staff as they get their new businesses up and running.

This is clearly a win-win partnership for both sides.

With a proven system, training and ongoing support, novices get a team of people to show them the way to success, helping them troubleshoot the rough spots along the way. As the IFA points out, with some franchise companies, the system is not dissimilar to the structure of military life.

While veterans can expect a little extra special treatment as thanks for their service to the country, franchise companies benefit from the particular strengths veterans bring to the franchise.

In its most recent survey, VetFran calculated that 238,000 veterans and military spouses have started careers in the franchise industry as either employees or owners. Since 2011, more than 6,500 veterans have become franchise business owners. Around one out of every seven franchise businesses are owned by a veteran of the US military, according to the IFA.

Here are some of the way's veterans are valued by franchisors.

The Treasured Traits of Veterans Prized by Franchisors

Integrity and Honor
Ingrained through their military training, veterans learn firsthand the importance of executing orders with dedication to accomplish a common goal.

Respect for Rules of Operation
Just like a military operation requires everyone to do his or her job, so does a franchise, which benefits when franchisees follow the proven system of the franchise company.

Leadership Training
Business ownership requires the type of leadership the military teaches. An owner is responsible for the business and its employees and, of course, is accountable to its customers.

Discipline
When the buck stops with you, you need a disciplined work ethic, especially during the early days as you build your business to profitability.

Character
Overcoming obstacles, an everyday activity for soldiers in the military, builds the kind of character necessary for business ownership.

Teamwork
In the military, soldiers learn to put the success of the mission ahead of their own interests. This dedication to teamwork suits the needs of franchisees to work with franchisors in a cooperative manner to maximize success.

Tech Savvy
The kind of expertise necessary to operate military hardware is likely miles ahead of the skills needed to operate an average franchise.

STORY FROM THE FIELD

The Advantage of Military Training When it Comes to Following a Franchise System

Succeeding with a franchise often comes down to whether you can and will follow the system, the essential sauce that likely attracted you to the franchise in the first place.

While learning and following the system can be challenging, one segment of the population is particularly well-suited to this aspect of franchising: military veterans, whose sense of mission tends to translate well to entrepreneurship.

"In the military, failure is not an option," explained Tammy Taylor, who served six years as a Navy corpsman. "When you take an oath, you're driven by the mission."

Taylor's sense of mission, combined with the discipline to make it work, and knowing deep in her bones that failure was not an option, proved a winning combination after she bought her franchise business, Always Best Care Senior Services, in 2011. All the qualities that allowed her to succeed as a Navy corpsman, helped her become Rookie of the Year.

For Taylor, 44, the call to service has been the drive she taps most, starting when she enlisted in the Navy during her senior year of high school when the country was engaged in the first Gulf War, Operation Desert Storm.

"I had at some level a calling," she said, adding that she was also influenced by her father's and grandfather's service in the military.

During her six years in the Navy, Taylor worked as a medical assistant, a bereavement counselor and became a nationally registered EMT. When she left, she brought her strong work ethic to corporate staffing in the pharmaceutical, technical (IT) and medical fields.

At her last job, she found herself traveling quite a bit and missing her three children, so she started looking around for what she could do in her local area, a New Jersey suburb of Philadelphia. At around that time, she recalls, she watched her father retire to be a caregiver for his parents and then become really run-down.

"I saw the impact of not having these resources…and an obvious need for services to support seniors," she said.

With the baby boomers entering their retirement years, Taylor realized the potential for growth in senior care, but she was primarily drawn to the work—the mission to help people cope with aging relatives.

After four months of research, she settled on Always Best Care (ABC), which provides non-medical in-home care. Taylor spent a great deal of time and effort thoroughly investigating the system and interviewing franchisees.

What clinched the decision was "I found that their people shared that same mission with me: they felt that sense of service," she explained.

At ABC she found a support network that helped her learn the system and, in turn, she brought her military discipline and commitment to make it all work even before the paycheck was there.

> "You have to have faith in the overall mission, your ability to prepare and complete it," she said. "This idea is ingrained in you in the military."

Another important lesson she learned in the military was how important each individual task is to the whole. If one element of the plan isn't executed, the whole mission can fall apart, and in the military, lives might be at stake. Every job is important, a critical lesson for good management and leadership.

Boot camp may have been her most important preparation for following a franchise system, she said.

"You know what to do and you do it," she explained. In a similar way, you don't want to overthink the system; you just do it. After you master the fundamentals, "You learn when to be a leader and when to follow the system."

Taylor always finds strength in the mission: "You remember why you're doing it, and I get to meet these wonderful people every day, and that's what keeps you going."

Six years into her business, Taylor says she still "loves everything about it. I can't imagine doing anything else."

NINE

Know How to Assess Profitability

Probably the first question that passes any business prospector's lips is: How much money can I make in this business? Arriving at a true answer, however, may not be as easy as it seems.

For starters, the question entails lots of unknown variables. First, as everyone knows, different people perform better with different models, depending on their skills, experience, and personalities. Some people, for example, are simply better able to adapt to changing circumstances and know how to take advantage of opportunities as they arise.

Second, and even more important, it takes time to get your business to profitability. How long varies, depending on internal, as well as external factors. One type of business might become profitable in just a month or two, while others can take several months. Getting to maximum profitability may take considerably longer, since the business will usually grow as you go along and gain knowledge and expertise. As I've mentioned, one of the biggest advantages of a franchise is that you can talk to franchisees, who can give you a good sense of how long a particular business takes to become profitable and how much profit you can eventually expect to make.

A good franchise system can show you how to bounce back from the rough spells and flourish every step along the way, from the first day through every evolutionary change in your industry. As we have emphasized, assessing whether your unique bundle of skills and experiences provides a good match for a specific business is a key part of your research.

Assuming you find a perfect franchise for your skill set, you like the executive team, you determine they have great training and support systems, and it's a business in which you can thrive, how much profit is enough?

To answer this important question, first you need to pose a set of basic questions to determine your own personal bottom line.

The Top Questions New Entrepreneurs Need to Ask Themselves

1. How Do I Balance Quality of Life with Earnings?

As you start to look around for a business to buy, you're likely thinking about the best ways to balance your life with your career. The good news is that with a franchise, you can find both high profit and work-life balance, whether that means flexible hours, fewer hours or the ability to work from home.

In the wide world of franchising, there is a category of franchise that requires fewer hours from the owner called semi-absentee. These businesses are set up to rely on a manager to run the business. The owner then manages the manager. Many semi-absentee businesses require only ten to fifteen hours per week from the owner, which makes them perfect for somebody looking for additional income while continuing with a job in the corporate world. This category can also suit the needs of someone looking to retire, yet not ready to stop working altogether.

2. Am I looking For a Six-Figure Income?

Almost every client I've ever had was looking for six figures, and some well into six figures. This is eminently possible with a franchise. But not all franchises will get you there. With the experience of a good franchise coach, plus a thorough due diligence process of your own that includes interviewing franchisees, you can get a good idea of what a franchisee can earn.

Of course, earnings will vary by owner. Some people are just better at running the business than others. Another point is some business types are not ever likely to earn more than five figures. If you plan and research correctly, however, there is no reason you can't pinpoint a business that has the potential to provide you the living you want.

3. Do I Want to Operate a Single-Unit or Multi-Unit Operation?

Many franchise companies allow you to earn well into the six figures with a single unit, but with other franchises, a six-figure income results from operating multiple units. In these franchises, each location is run by a hired manager, which allows you to acquire and operate several sites.

These franchises can be extremely lucrative. If you see yourself owning multiple locations and you're willing to accept that your earnings will only build to their highest level as you open your second or third, then this type of franchise might be a good fit for you. Many people do extraordinarily well with large numbers of locations. Of course, by then you will have developed a crack administrative team to help you manage them all.

4. The Smartest Question: How Much Money Do I Need to Get Going?

When you embark on a new business venture, let me reiterate, the single most important question to ask yourself is: How much capital will I need? Even with the best idea in the world, if you can't keep your business going while you get all your systems up and running, you'll go under.

In short, you need capital to get you through the start-up phase.

Virtually the only business model where you can definitively answer the question, "How much money do I need?" is a franchise, whose systems and capital requirements have been tested by dozens of franchisees.

You can find out how much it costs to start up and operate in the franchise company's Financial Disclosure Document (FDD), which all franchisors are required by federal law to provide to potential franchisees.

Besides learning all your upfront costs ahead of time, you can and should learn about potential costs by interviewing franchisees. Don't forget to factor in differences based on geography and the range of talents and skills of individual franchisees.

Even armed with the knowledge about how much it will cost to run your business, you should figure out how much money you need to live on until your business starts generating income.

Some franchise companies will disclose earnings estimates, but you should always double and triple-check these numbers with franchisees. A realistic, even conservative, estimate is essential. Your success may depend on it.

3 Keys to Understanding Your Potential Earnings

Know Your Timetable
Most businesses take at least a couple of months to start earning a profit. The slowest to become profitable are franchises that take longer to build a customer base. If the margins are thinner, you need to generate more volume.

Accurately Estimate Your Start-Up Costs
The FDD provides a list of all your start-up costs, which are far more extensive than just the initial franchise fee. Item 7 gives you the actual numbers for costs and includes signage, office furniture, equipment, leases and security deposits, licenses and permits.

Estimate Potential Income
Flip now to Item 19 of the FDD to read if the franchisor has made any earnings claims. Only about one-third of franchisors make earnings claims, and how franchise companies address this issue varies.

To fill out the picture, you will need to call as many franchisees as it takes to learn reliable answers to your questions, preferably those operating in locations like yours, to verify all the information in the FDD and get an idea on profits. Word to the wise, avoid the question: How much money do you earn? Instead, try a softer approach, such as: "How long until I can expect to make $100,000?" Then try out different numbers.

Financing a Franchise

Your top priority must be ensuring you have enough money to start and run your business until you begin to earn a profit.

As we have emphasized, by the time you invest capital into your new business, you should know from your research and preparation exactly how much money you will need, and you should be certain that the business you select matches your skills, experience and interest.

Many lending options are available to finance new franchise businesses, even though most are purchased by people who have never run a business before and usually are new to the particular business. The reason: Franchises offer a proven model for earning profits.

Most franchisees put together a package that may include:

- A loan from the US Small Business Association (SBA)
- Traditional savings
- Home equity loan
- Tapping into a 401K or IRA

While using retirement funds to help you start a new business should not be undertaken lightly, the procedure, called Rollover as Business Startups, has many advantages, according to Sherri Seiber, chief operating officer of FranFund Inc., a Fort Worth, Tex.-based firm that has advised thousands of franchisees on funding their new businesses.

This technique, nicknamed ROBS by FranFund, allows you to self-fund your new business by using your retirement funds, pay no tax on the funds you use, and save the costs associated with a loan.

Seiber, who jokes about the ironic acronym, said the Employee Retirement Income Security Act of 1974 allows people to roll over a portion or all of their 401K or IRA (not Roth IRA) into a new 401K profit-sharing plan sponsored by your new corporation or business entity, which buys stock in the new corporation without penalty or paying additional tax.

The 401K becomes a stockholder in the new business. The operating account of this new corporation can be used for any legitimate business expense, including paying yourself a salary during the start-up phase before you begin generating revenue.

Instead of your 401K buying stock or mutual funds, you use your retirement savings to invest in your business. If the value of your business increases, so does your retirement account. Likewise, if, in the worst-case scenario, your business fails, you lose your money, but you won't have tax liabilities and penalties. And unlike traditional loans, you wouldn't be putting collateral, such as a house, at risk.

ROBS had been a top way businesses under $150,000 to $200,000 got funded a few years back, Seiber said. "Back then, 65 percent to 70 percent of our clients used that method alone or in conjunction with another loan."

But as credit has loosened up as we get further past the Great Recession, Seiber noted, only about 55 percent of their clients use ROBS to finance their businesses, and many are combined with a loan.

Some people use ROBS as a way to inject equity into a loan application.

The main caveat is that you could lose your retirement savings, and as Seiber notes, if you don't believe you can be successful in your new business, this path is probably not for you—and, of course, you may not want to go into that business at all.

If you don't want to touch your retirement account, bank lending can be a good alternative, particularly as lending markets have opened up after years of limited activity following the Great Recession.

"We have a group of lenders who like franchises," Seiber said, and FranFund can often get people with good credit through the approval process in under five days.

FranFund's specialty is putting together a complete package that can move quickly through the process for a "fast and reliable yes."

Many firms offer ways to prequalify people for loans, which can help speed up the application.

There is one final question you have to ask yourself:

> *Do you really believe you have what it takes—*
> *meaning skills, experience, and work ethic—to*
> *to make a success of your new business?*

If the answer is yes, then you can feel comfortable investing in yourself.

Experts are Essential! Consult an Attorney and an Accountant

In our increasingly complex economy, most people occupy ever more specialized niches. Take heart—no one knows it all. Which is precisely why you shouldn't shy away from starting your own business. There's an expert for everything you need to know to succeed. Besides, as we've been saying, with a franchise, you get a whole back room full of experts to help you succeed with your business.

On the other hand, it's your job to protect your own finances before you sign any contracts. This is why we advise our clients to consult with experts to help protect their interests. And yes, you will have to pay their fees, but count this as insurance against making mistakes that can cost you a whole lot more down the line.

The most important expert to help you save a world of regret later is a lawyer. But not just anyone will do. You need to find an attorney who is an expert in franchising.

Consult an Attorney

Just as you wouldn't hire a civil attorney to defend you in criminal court, if you want assistance on buying a franchise, consult attorneys who make this their specialty.

We highly recommend you consult a franchise attorney, one who has read hundreds of franchise contracts and FDDs, one who can help you recognize potential pitfalls and figure out ways to protect your investment.

A franchise Attorney Will Help You:
Understand the meaning of the documents you are going to sign, especially as they impact your obligations as a franchise owner.

Obtain clarification amendments to the documents. Franchise companies will not allow material modifications to the franchise agreements. They will, however, often allow you to insert language clarifying the agreement's meaning to ensure your rights are unambiguous.

Consult an Accountant
Just as you would never attempt to read up on the law, so you could avoid hiring an attorney, you should not try to fast-track an accounting course to help you make smart financial decisions for your business.

The entrepreneur has two main accounting issues to consider.

You Need to be Smart About:

- ✓ How to finance your business *and*
- ✓ How you manage operations. Good mechanisms for measuring key indices of your business can help you correct errors early and capitalize on strengths.

Accountants bring essential expertise drawn from experience working with hundreds or thousands of other businesses before you.

As mentioned, numerous times, the most common reason a new business might fail is due to insufficient capitalization. As a result, managing cash flow may be your most important responsibility even if it has nothing to do with your core ideas, talents or skills. And that's the point. Hire an accountant. How are you going to know if you actually have the next big thing if you can't make it through the start-up phase?

The Bottom Line of Your Due Diligence

The best source of information on buying a franchise are franchisees themselves, the folks who did their due diligence, and took the time upfront to research the best franchise for their own set of skills and experience. They found that running their own businesses offered them a path to greater contentment than their former lives tied to corporate jobs, where the odds of getting laid off or downsized increases with time.

Over the years, I have worked with thousands of people interested in learning more about owning their own business and have monitored hundreds who made the educated decision to become entrepreneurs. As someone who has operated independent businesses, as well as franchise businesses, I feel strongly that a franchise is by far the best way to minimize your risk on the path to becoming an entrepreneur.

Still, nothing makes the point better than stories from the field.

No-Nonsense Advice

Over the years and the many conversations I've had with would-be and experienced franchisees I have developed a list of no-nonsense advice that distills the best of their cumulative wisdom for success.

Franchisees' Formula for Success:

- **Take your time and do your research.**
  The point has been made!

- **Be guided by research.**
  One of the most common errors people make is to reject a franchise because the business did not seem interesting. This is a mistaken premise. After all, with most franchises, you will work on the business, not in the business.

  You may, for example, quite enjoy the business of running a hair salon, which includes executing an advertising campaign, delegating to the manager and researching the real-estate market for your next location, even if you have no interest in cutting hair.

- **Understand your own capabilities.**
  Do a personal assessment before choosing a franchise.

- **Establish a realistic business plan.**
  Imagine best-case as well as worst-case scenarios and make sure you can manage in a worse-case scenario, which might include snafus in pricing, marketing, or staffing. These kinds of kinks can be worked out with the help of quality support from a good franchise company.

- **Follow the plan.**
  One key part of your upfront research is to determine if the franchisor's operational plan works. If you believe it does, and then you decide to invest in the franchise, you are investing in that plan.

Be aware: It will take time to reach profitability, and you will have challenges along the way. During discouraging moments, you need to remain steady and keep in mind that your own research determined the plan is sound. Stay conscious of that fact, and then stick to the plan. Let me repeat: **Stick to the plan!**

Running Your Own Business is the Best Way to Control the Future of Your Career

It has become clear that yesterday's corporate world is gone. No longer do employers nurture management to encourage long-term careers of twenty years or more. Your HR department is no longer on your side, helping you navigate your career progression. If you want to have control over the future of your career, the best way is to own your own business.

A Franchise Gives You Access to a Fruitful Partnership

A good franchisor provides you with all the expertise you need to start your business and succeed. Let the miscellaneous details get handled by the back office while you work on building your business. The key to this method is finding a good franchise, which is why spending so much time on research is step number one.

The payoff:
You get to be your own boss.
You get to manage your own time.
You get to keep the profits.

TEN

Conclusion

By now, you've likely absorbed the key lesson we've tried to convey: Owning a successful business is more realistic than most people think. And you're likely serious about taking steps to recharge your career. As you've learned from the stories about successful mid-career entrepreneurs, making the change is not a risk to be avoided, but rather a decision you should seriously consider so long as you can commit to following the process that reduces your risk.

To take the next step—committing to the process—I'll repeat a phrase I used in the introduction:

Successful Entrepreneurs Seize Opportunities While Minimizing Risk

Mustering the courage to take advantage of an opportunity becomes infinitely easier once you realize you have all the tools you need to reduce your risk. In addition, your incentive increases once you fully understand the substantial upside to owning your own business. As you have seen, with your own business you get:

- An opportunity for increased wealth and income
- Freedom and flexibility over your life and your job
- The chance to renew your passion and enthusiasm for your career
- Control over the future of your career and
- Greater stability with less career risk

When considering this type of career change, remember, you won't have to work any harder than you do in your current job. With your own business, you can focus your work on advancing your goals, gaining greater career satisfaction, increasing your income and your bottom line. How great is that!

As I have written and stated in numerous seminars, speeches, and webinars, you don't have to reinvent the wheel to own a thriving business. You can get a great business model, created and honed by hundreds of entrepreneurs who came before you, complete with a back room full of expertise and all the tools you need to succeed, plus a great network of support. All it takes is making the right match, which—make no mistake—requires you to complete your due diligence and use every resource available to you to help ensure you select a business that truly is right for you.

I know I sound like a broken record when I talk about research. The reason is simple: In the process of selecting the best franchise to give you the future of your dreams, there's nothing more important than research.

While people may say they understand that research is important, most people don't do a fraction of what is actually necessary. There's a big difference between calling one or two franchisees and calling ten or fifteen. I had one client who called every single franchisee on the list. She got her new franchise up and running quickly and was drawing a paycheck in just weeks. She was not surprised because her thorough research had given her the knowledge to make this happen.

What is absolutely essential is a realistic and accurate appraisal of your abilities. Don't force yourself out of your comfort zone or try to mold yourself to suit a particular business. If you hate sales, don't buy a business that includes a large component of cold calling. You have enough business choices. You can and should choose a business that suits your personality and skills. After all, when you become an entrepreneur, you want to love going to work every day.

Over the years, I've found the top reasons for franchise failure are totally within your control and easy to avoid.

Likewise, the ability to succeed is also within your control. The key to buying and succeeding with a franchise can be summed up in two steps:

1. Do your due diligence.
2. Follow the system.

The only thing you can know for certain is that change is always coming. Why not take those first baby steps and investigate your options? Take charge of your career and get the life you always wanted.

Ready to Proceed?

If you want to start the coaching process with us, the first step is to complete our Entrepreneur Assessment, which you can find at:

http://tinyurl.com/teoassessment

GLOSSARY

Dan's *Redefining* of Words

Here's a different way of looking at terms used in this book. While certainly not the definitions you will find in Webster's, these definitions are my way of cutting through corporate America's tendency to use euphemisms.

Age Discrimination – The truth behind the lies you are told when you are terminated or passed over.

Assumptions – Beliefs we make that hide the truth from us.

Bureaucracy – What large corporations use to take all the fun out of working.

Career – That job you used to enjoy, but which now feels like a joyless trap.

Control – The thing your boss has over you if you are an employee. What an employee does not have over their schedule, pay, or future.

Discipline – A determined focus on what needs to be done. For employees, this benefits their employers. For business owners, this benefits themselves.

Downsizing – When a corporation decides to fire groups of loyal, hard-working employees so that the bosses can keep their jobs. One of several code words that corporate America has come up with to hide the harshness of its actions.

Due Diligence – The research process you go through when evaluating a franchise. Something you want to do in great depth before you decide to invest. The thing you are able to do to a far greater extent with a franchise than with any other type of business. The way you get answers to your questions.

Entrepreneur – A person taking advantage of a business opportunity. Someone with the desire for the upside that comes from business ownership but not the downside that comes from reckless risk.

Experience – The hard-won attribute you possess that can help you thrive in business ownership.

Facts – Information that is true, but unseen by many due to their fears or assumptions.

Failure – The number one outcome that you do not want from your new business. The outcome you are unlikely to experience with a franchise if you complete a thorough due-diligence and follow the franchise system.

Family – Those people who love and support you and will "have your back" as you start your business. Those whom you will be able to spend more time with once you achieve more flexibility in your work. Those who will benefit from a better lifestyle when your new business increases your income.

Fast Food – The thing most people think of when they see the word franchise. Actually, it comprises less than 5 percent of franchises.

Fear – Unreal impediments that hide actual opportunities, often based on false assumptions.

Flexibility – The ability to choose your own schedule, decide on your own vacation dates, and make last minute changes. It's possessed by bosses and business owners but denied to most employees.

Franchise – A way to own a business that reduces risk. Comes with unique benefits that enable you to learn all about it before you invest anything at all. It includes a full set of instructions on how to run your business.

Franchise coach – An experienced professional who can help you get the things you want from your work life.

Franchise Disclosure Document (FDD) – Legal, written information every franchise company must provide if you are considering buying that franchise. The best starting place to get key, informative details on the franchise.

Franchisee – This could be you, after completing thorough due diligence, which allows you to discover a great company with a business that is a good fit for you.

Franchisor – The parent company that trains you and supports you from beginning to end when you own a franchise. The company that employs the people who give you help.

Independence – What people yearn for. Not available to employees in corporate America.

Job – A frustrating place employees must go to every day, where they create money and accolades for their employer.

Layoff – See Downsizing.

Mid-Career – That place where you feel uninspired and stuck.

Millionaire – Usually, people who own their own businesses.

Money – Something most often obtained in quantity only by people who own their own business. Something chased but rarely caught by employees.

Office Politics – The games people play that you just don't enjoy. Behavior that people with less talent than you sometimes use to become your boss.

Owner – The one who gets to keep the profits. The one who gets to make decisions. The one who has the flexible schedule.

Perspective – An outlook you can shift so you see what is actually there, instead of what unfounded fears cause you to think you see.

Profit – What a successful business creates. In all cases, this belongs to the owners of the business, not to the people who do the work.

Red Tape – See Bureaucracy.

Reduction in Force (RIF) – See Downsizing.

Responsibility – What your boss takes for the things you have done well. Also, what your boss assigns to you for problems.

Research – See Due Diligence.

Retirement – That far-away dream that two-thirds of people over the age of 50 believe they will never be able to afford.

Risk – The possibility of a downside you can refuse to accept when you own a business. Oddly, concerns about this fictitious beast are the number one reason people choose a career other than business ownership. (See assumptions.)

Salary – The amount of money your boss decides to give you for your work. A quantity far less than what you contribute to the corporate bottom line.

Semi-absentee – A kind of business where the owner manages a manager. In this format, the owner does little of the hands-on work and keeps all the profit.

Skills – The valuable abilities you have learned through training and experience. For employees, these benefit their employers. For business owners these benefit themselves.

Success – What you want but can't seem to find enough of. What your boss seems to have, but for you stays just out of reach. It includes money, control, independence, balance, and flexibility.

Three years – The average length of employment before your boss tells you to leave. A time allotment that has no relationship to the quality of work you do.

Unreasonable Demands – A thing your boss gets to make.

Validation – The part of your due diligence process where you talk to existing franchise owners. These owners are the ones who can tell you what it's really like to be a franchisee. It allows you to get the truth from people who actually know it.

Work Ethic – A willingness to do the hard stuff. For most people, this benefits their employers. For business owners, this benefits themselves

Work-Life Balance – Believed to be a myth by employees of large corporations. An actual benefit for business owners who prioritize it.

END NOTES

Part I

Chapter 1: The Connection Between Control & Happiness

1. Hoskins, Diane, "Employees Perform Better When They can Control Their Own Space," *Harvard Business Review*. (Online, 16 Jan. 2014)

Chapter 2: The Upside of Starting Your Own Business

2. Kauffman Foundation and Legal Zoom, "Who Started New Businesses in 2013?" *Online*. (January 2014)

3. Merrill Lynch, "Work in Retirement: Myths and Motivations: Career Reinventions and the New Retirement Workscape," *A Merrill Lynch Retirement Study conducted in partnership with Age Wave*. (2014)

4. Wells Fargo Survey Finds Saving for Retirement Not Happening for a Third of Middle Class: More than Half Plan to Save "Later" to Make up for Lost Ground." *News Release. Online*. (22 Oct 2014)

5. Tergesen, Anne. "The Case for Quitting Your Job Even if You Love It, Walking Away Might Leave You Healthier and Happier." *Wall Street Journal*. (13 Oct. 2014.)

APPENDICES

I
Franchise Categories

II
Self-Assessment

III
Self-Evaluation Worksheet

IV
Key Questions to Ask Franchisees

V
Key Questions to Ask Franchisors

APPENDIX I

Franchise Categories

The following franchise categories represent a sample of some of the types of franchises available. This should start to give you a feel for your individual interests.

AUTOMOTIVE	
☐ Customizing	☐ Interior Restoration
☐ Body Work & Painting	☐ Tires
☐ General Repair	☐ Wash & Detail
BUSINESS SERVICES	
☐ Accounting	☐ Expense Reduction Consulting
☐ Advertising & Direct Mail	☐ Large Format Graphics, Printing
☐ Business Coaching	☐ Office Support Services
☐ Business Consulting	☐ Pack, Ship, Copying Services
☐ Business Development Services	☐ Professional ☐ Window Cleaning
☐ Commercial Cleaning	☐ Property Management
☐ Computer & IT Services	☐ Restaurant Support Services
☐ Employee Drug Testing	☐ Sales Training
☐ Executive Training	☐ Salon Development ☐ & Rental
☐ Executive Recruiting	☐ Sign Manufacturing
	☐ Temp Staffing
CHILD CARE / EDUCATION	
☐ Activities & Sports	☐ Learning Center
☐ After-school Programs	☐ Recreation
☐ Art & Cooking	☐ Tutoring
	☐ STEM

CONSUMER SERVICES

☐ Air Duct Cleaning	☐ Home Improvement
☐ Beauty Services	☐ Home Repair & Maintenance
☐ Cell Phone Repair	☐ Lawn Care
☐ Closet & Garage Organizing	☐ Massage & Spa
☐ Day Care	☐ Medical Services
☐ Disaster Recovery	☐ Mobility Equipment
☐ Exterior Home & Yard Services	☐ Painting
☐ Fitness & Exercise	☐ Pet Services
☐ Health Enhancement	☐ Pet Supplies
☐ House Cleaning	☐ Senior Care
☐ Junk Removal & Hauling	☐ Weight Loss
☐ Hair Salon	

FOOD

☐ Catering	☐ Healthy Foods & Smoothies
☐ Coffee & Tea	☐ Ice Cream & Frozen Yogurt
☐ Desserts & Baked Goods	☐ Pizza
☐ Global Foods	☐ Restaurants

RETAIL

☐ Consignment Stores	☐ Pet Food & Supplies
☐ Custom T-Shirt	☐ Women's Boutique
☐ Electronics & IT	☐ Children's Items

APPENDIX II

Self-Assessment

PART I – PERSONAL INFORMATION			
Name:			
Address:			
City:	State:		Zip Code:
Cell #:	Home #:		Work #:
E-Mail:	DOB:		
Relationship Status: ☐ Single ☐ Married ☐ Divorced ☐ Widowed ☐ Other			
Partner's Name:		# of Dependents:	
Partner's Occupation:			
Own or Rent Home?		# Years:	
U.S. Citizen?		Veteran?	
Education: ☐ High School ☐ Bachelors ☐ Masters ☐ PhD ☐ Other			
Current or most recent occupation?			
Current or most recent employer?			
Most recent income: $			
Have you ever owned a business?			
If Yes, what type?			
How strong is your desire to own our own business? 1-10			
How long have you been looking for a business?			
What types of businesses have you looked into?			

What are the preferred locations (cities) for your business?	
1.	
2.	
3.	

PART II – BUSINESS CONSIDERATIONS

What was your FAVORITE part of your last job or business?
What was your LEAST favorite part of your last job or business?
What do you consider your GREATEST business achievement?
What are your strengths?
What are your weaknesses?
What are your hobbies and interests?
Do you like working with your hands?
Do you own pets?
How would you rate your sales ability? 1-10
How would you rate your interest in sales? 1-10
Will family members be involved in the business? If so, whom?
Will you be in involved in the business: ☐ Full-Time   ☐ Part-Time

My Ideal business would like something like this:

Business location is based at: ☐ Facility   ☐ Home   ☐ No preference
Customer purchasing pattern: ☐ Repeat   ☐ Anytime   ☐ No preference
Do you prefer your customer to be: ☐ Business   ☐ Consumer   ☐ No p Preference
Number of Employees: ☐ 10+   ☐ 5-9   ☐ 0-4
Do you prefer to provide: ☐ Product   ☐ Service   ☐ Both
Who will make the decision?   ☐ Self   ☐ Spouse   ☐ Other
Your need for personal income within: ☐ 3-6 mo.   ☐ 6-9 mo.   ☐ 1 Year
Amount of income you will need within the above time frame?

PART III – CONFIDENTIAL FINANCIAL INFORMATION

ASSETS	LIABILITIES
Cash	Notes Payable to Bank
Stocks & Bonds	Notes Payable, other
IRA	Credit Card

401K	Finance Companies
Home Value	Mortgage, home
Real Estate, other	Mortgage, other
Other Assets	Taxes
Total Assets	**Total Liabilities**

Net Worth	Liquid Capital
Your investment	Amount to Finance
Do you have a financial partner or other source of investment capital?	
Would you like help with exploring funding options?	

APPENDIX III

Self-Evaluation Worksheet
Career Experiences

As discussed in Part I, disconnect your skills from your job title. For example, rather than list accounting as the one and only skill, break down the job into its component parts: i.e., good numbers sense, time management, public speaker, etc. Refer to the list of "General Business Skills" below and see **PART I, CHAPTER 3** for additional ideas.

General Business Skills

Leadership
Having the ability to recruit, motivate and retain good employees

Managing Employees
- Building a high-performing team
- Mentoring and coaching employees
- Keep them working to achieve your vision

Marketing Promotion
Developing your business in the local and regional community

Networking
Developing relationships with key local partners

Communication
Writing, explaining, listening, interpreting

Public Speaking	*Negotiating*
Problem Solving	*Project Management*
Analysis	*Financial Management*

Entrepreneur's Checklist

How do you interact in a business situation? Are you:
- ☐ Detail oriented
- ☐ A big-picture thinker
- ☐ Good at follow-through
- ☐ A people person

Do you have:
- ☐ Sufficient drive
- ☐ Faith in your ability to make things happen
- ☐ Independence
- ☐ Emotional resilience
- ☐ Comfort with uncertainty
- ☐ A willingness to follow a system
- ☐ Sufficient capital
- ☐ Support of family, especially your spouse!

APPENDIX IV

Key Questions to Ask Franchisees

You may ask franchisees as many questions as you wish, however, we suggest the questions below are key and should not be missed. It is important to keep in mind that franchisees have no ulterior agenda, and no reason to mislead you. They are independent, and if they have any issues with the franchisor, they will usually let you know.

Franchisees are not obligated to talk to you, so don't expect every one of them to call you back. They are busy running their business. If you have trouble contacting a specific individual, consider emailing them to set up a convenient time to talk.

FRANCHISEE QUESTIONS	
FRANCHISE:	**DATE:**
OWNER NAME:	**LOCATION:**
Have you been satisfied with the level of ongoing support from the franchisor?	
Did you find your training substantial?	
What was your professional background?	
What made you choose this franchise?	
What do you like best and least about the business?	
How long have you been in business?	
About how long did it take you to reach profitability?	
If franchisee is new, ask if they are on plan to reach profitability.	
Does this franchise have the potential for a franchisee to earn in the six-figure range? If so, how long should that take?	
Your net income is approximately what percent of your revenue?	
Approximately how much per year do you spend for:	
Advertising & Marketing:	Rent / Utilities:

Insurance:	Employee Wages:
Other:	
How difficult is it to find employees?	
How are the employees compensated?	
Do you provide benefits?	
How would you rate the franchisor's marketing programs and tools?	
How would you rate your relationship with the franchisor?	
Going back in time, would you buy this franchise again?	
ADDITIONAL QUESTIONS & NOTES	

APPENDIX V

Key Questions to Ask Franchisors

FRANCHISOR QUESTIONS	
FRANCHISE:	**DATE:**
CONTACT:	**PHONE #:**
How many years have you been franchising?	
How many franchisees do you currently have?	
How many of these franchisees own multiple locations?	
How many new units are expected over the next 3 years?	
How many units, if any, have closed over the past five years?	
Have there been any lawsuits or arbitration actions?	
How would you describe the level of satisfaction by the majority of your franchisees?	
How do most franchisees describe their relationship with you?	
FRANCHISEE SUPPORT	
How long is your initial training?	
What do you do to train franchisees on an ongoing basis?	
Which of the following do you provide for your franchisees?	
Annual Meetings	Field Support
Purchasing Assistance	Strategic Planning Assistance
Call Center	Marketing Support
FRANCHISEE OBLIGATIONS	
What is the ongoing % royalty?	
What is the initial license fee?	
What is the advertising fee?	

Do you have any other ongoing fees?
What is the total initial investment?
How much working capital do you recommend?
Do you have an Item 19 earnings claim in your FDD?
What does the franchise owner focus their time on?

THE FRANCHISE SYSTEM

Do you have proprietary software for running the franchise?
Do you have proprietary equipment?
What are the advantages of your system over competitors?
Who are your major competitors?

MANAGEMENT

Who are the key executives in the franchise and what are their backgrounds?
How long has the current management team been in place?

FRANCHISE FINANCIAL POSITION

Is the franchise company publicly traded?
How much revenue is received from franchise fees?
How much revenue from royalty payments?
Other comments on financial position:

ADDITIONAL QUESTIONS & NOTES

ABOUT THE AUTHOR

Dan Citrenbaum has spent his entire career as an entrepreneur and, over the past four decades, has helped thousands of people realize their dreams of business ownership.

Since entering the world of franchising, Dan has achieved his own goals and helped others achieve theirs as well. As a franchise coach with **The Entrepreneur Option**, Dan has assisted thousands of people to learn about franchises, from how to conduct a thorough due diligence to discovering if a franchise business is right for them.

When he purchased an Area Representative franchise in **Always Best Care Senior Services®**, he grew his territory to the company's number one in the world. He also coached and supported franchisees in Always Best Care. The small group of franchise owners he worked with at Always Best Care twice won both Franchisee of the Year and Rookie of the year.

After 11 years of ownership, Dan sold his Always Best Care back to the franchise company in 2021. After having earned millions of dollars during the time he owned his business, he sold it for millions more.

More recently, Dan added **The Groutsmith™** franchise to his portfolio, quickly growing that business to profitability. His franchise is one of the fastest growing in the The Groutsmith™ system.